The Compleat Guide to Day Trading Stocks

The Compleat Guide to Day Trading Stocks

Jake Bernstein

McGraw-Hill, Inc.

New York   San Francisco   Washington, D.C.   Auckland   Bogotá
Caracas   Lisbon   London   Madrid   Mexico City   Milan
Montreal   New Delhi   San Juan   Singapore
Sydney   Tokyo   Toronto

Library of Congress Cataloging-in-Publication Data

Bernstein, Jacob
   The compleat guide to day trading stocks / by Jake Bernstein.
      p. cm.
   Includes bibliographical references.
   ISBN 0-07-136125-1
   1. Day trading (Securities)   2. Electronic trading of securities. I. Title.
HG4515.95 .B468 2000
332.64′0285—dc21

                                                  00-040102

McGraw-Hill

*A Division of The **McGraw·Hill** Companies*

1 2 3 4 5 6 7 8 9 0 PBT/PBT 0 9 8 7 6 5 4 3 2 1 0

ISBN 0-07-136125-1

This book was set in Palatino by North Market Street Graphics.

Printed and bound by Phoenix Book Technologies.

This publication is designed to provide accurate and authoritative information in regard to the subject matter covered. It is sold with the understanding that the publisher is not engaged in rendering legal, accounting, or other professional service. If legal advice or other expert assistance is required, the services of a competent professional person should be sought.

> *—From a declaration of principles jointly adopted by a committee of the American Bar Association and a committee of publishers.*

 This book is printed on recycled, acid-free paper containing a minimum of 50% recycled de-inked fiber.

McGraw-Hill books are available at special quantity discounts to use as premiums and sales promotions, or for use in corporate training programs. For more information, please write to the Director of Special Sales, Professional Publishing, McGraw-Hill, Two Penn Plaza, New York, NY 10121. Or contact your local bookstore.

This book is dedicated to day traders and aspiring day traders the world over. Your task is arduous; your challenge immense. The promise of victory and lure of wealth inspire you daily to confront the odds of success.

I give you this book in the hope that my efforts, research, suggestions, systems, and methods will help you achieve your goals.

Contents

Preface

There was a time when day trading was considered the realm of the market specialist, the professional trader, or the extreme risk taker. Most day trading was restricted to the futures markets where margin requirements were in the 1 percent to 3 percent range and intraday price movements were large and frequent. Markets like pork belly futures, soybean futures, Treasury bond futures, currency futures, and stock index futures were the domain of the day trader. But time passes and things change! High-flying technology stocks are the pork bellies of today's day trader in securities. In fact, the term *security* is an oxymoron when used in reference to day trading stocks. The simple truth is that day trading in stocks is at times more speculative than day trading in the commodity futures markets.

In the late 1960s, when I was a college student at the University of Illinois, a good friend convinced me to open a stock trading account at what was then the Hayden-Stone brokerage office in Champaign, Illinois. Although John was too young to open an account, he was nonetheless a consummate stock market analyst. Schooled in part by his father, a man whose experience dated back to the Great Depression era, John was exceptionally knowledgeable about stocks, market trends, market history, technical analysis, fundamental analysis, and more. I lost contact with John many years ago. Still, I think back fondly on those days and regret only that I failed to learn even more from him about stock analysis than I did.

It took a considerable amount of convincing and badgering before I opened an account. I bought 100 shares of Wright Hargeaves (WRT), a Canadian gold producer. As I recall, WRT was trading at about $2 or $3 per share. John, a dedicated "gold bug," was convinced that gold would one day explode and our meager investment in WRT would bring great profits. Of course, gold wasn't our only interest. We graduated to mobile home stocks such as Fleetwood Enterprises and DMH (Detroit Mobile Home), semiconductor manufacturers such as Texas Instruments, and high-tech medical stocks such as Medtronic and the promising National Patent Development. But I was brainwashed and raised on gold shares.

Several times daily, either on my way to or from classes or (I admit) instead of classes, I found myself at the Hayden-Stone office watching the ticker tape. Every $\frac{1}{16}$-point rise in WRT stock cheered me. Every $\frac{1}{16}$-point decline caused me chagrin. I listened (only half-heartedly, I confess) to John's preachings about gold, the gold standard, the eroding state of world economies, the inevitable and unavoidable collapse of the U.S. dollar, and the concomitant rise of precious metals. But John was insistent on one major point: *in a rising market most stocks will rise and in a falling market most stocks will fall.* Simple as this may sound, it is a lesson that many investors and traders today fail to understand. And it is a truism we will revisit often in this book.

Weeks passed and WRT moved in our favor by a mere ¾ of a point. Yet this was cause for celebration. Let us not forget that in the late 1960s, "a dollar was a dollar." During the preinflation era of the 1960s, one could buy a new Volkswagen for about $1600. In the year 2000, a new Beetle costs more than 10 times that! And so our mere 100 shares of WRT in today's market might be valued at $30 per share. Still, trading in WRT failed to satisfy my need (as well as John's) to make it big in the market. While John continued his intensive studies of the stock market, I moved on to the highly speculative commodity futures markets. And John also explored the commodity markets, since this was where the real action was.

Short-term trading and day trading were common in the commodity markets. But day trading in stocks was not considered a worthwhile venture for the average investor. It was, rather, something that professional stock traders, market makers, floor specialists, and extremely wealthy investors could do. After all, stocks rarely made large intraday moves. It was therefore necessary to trade large numbers of shares to make money. Furthermore, the cost of commissions was prohibitively high, making the day trade generally unfeasible for the average trader. In short, the way to make money in stocks was to buy low and sell high, holding for a relatively lengthy period. At times the more speculative and higher-priced stocks were reasonable day-trading or short-term trading vehicles but there were numerous obstacles, not the least of which was the need to have a live stock ticker. But the cost of a ticker was also a major factor. Yes, one could sit at the brokerage house and trade stocks all day, but then that luxury was reserved for the independently wealthy.

In short, day trading stocks was not a viable venture for a student, a new investor, or a person of limited financial means. The best strategy was to invest in stocks for the long term. "Buy and hold," "buy low and sell high," or "buy high and sell higher" were the prevailing methods of making money in stocks. But in order to achieve these goals one had to give the market time. Stocks moved slowly, and traders had no choice but to follow the slow lead of stocks. Those who were frustrated with the lack of movement could either become market specialists, "swing a big line" (i.e., trade large numbers of shares for small moves), or trade commodities.

Yes, things have changed. Now we can day trade thousands of shares of stocks for one commission. We can get stock quotes virtually free of charge. And we can place orders instantly without the need of a broker. We live in an age of "instantism." As I will point out later in this book, the philosophical merit of immediacy and instant gratification or feedback is one which can and should be considered, debated, evaluated, and seriously analyzed in terms of its appropriateness to you, the trader.

While "instantism" may be the leitmotif of today's trader, the zeitgeist of our times, this does not mean ipso facto that it is the best thing for all of us. Some of us prefer slowness. Some of us prefer time to think, to evaluate, to analyze, and to make decisions unfettered by the pressure of the moment. We enjoy the luxury of methodical mental market meanderings. Some of us prefer the low-tech world of paper and pencil, of manually updated charts, to keyboard, mouse, and screen.

There are those who will claim that slowness is incompatible with profitable day trading. And they may be right. Yet to the surprise of many relatively new traders, the knowledge and experience gained in a lifetime of trading without computers can still afford the trader an inexplicable edge which cannot be acquired by burying one's nose in a computer screen, Internet Web site, or software program. Does this mean that I am opposed to the modern-day tools that can make profitable day trading in stocks a reality? No, not at all! My statement is merely intended to give another perspective, to perhaps give you food for thought in order to determine what is truly right for you as a trader or investor.

As you read this book, I urge you to keep foremost in mind your goals and their cost to your quality of life. Is the game worth the candle? Is success as a day trader worth the stress and risk of loss and the pressure to produce? Is the game truly satisfying? Are you better off sitting in front of a computer screen day trading shares in companies whose businesses are intangible or would you be best off high over a woodland, as a ranger, standing watch over a national forest? Yes, these are the kinds of philosophical, personal, spiritual, and metaphysical questions you will rarely see raised in a book such as this.

After all, day trading is a mercenary thing. It is generally thought to be incompatible with deep philosophical thought. We assume (right or wrong) that philosophers, romantics, and deep thinkers have no need for money. They seem to survive on very little, while those who succeed in the world of finance are godless, thoughtless, ruthless, mercenary, Machiavellian, manipulating, shameless schemers. I vehemently disagree. If you want to succeed as a day trader (or for that matter, as anything else) then you must first look within. Clean the house of your mind and soul, and then the path will be clearer. Your road to success will be unencumbered by thorny issues whose branches impede your passage. If you want to succeed at any venture or adventure in the outer world, make certain that your inner world is in order.

What Makes This Book Different?

There are many books you can buy on day trading. As of this writing, there are at least 40 books available on day trading—and the list is growing. What makes this book different from the others? Why spend your time reading what I have to say? Here is my list of the reasons, simply, succinctly, and without excessive verbiage.

- This is one of the few books that give you exact strategies for stock day trading. I also offer you a look at the techniques and strategies of day trading rounded out by a clear explanation of what it takes emotionally and psychologically to succeed at the game. Far too many books throw information at you, expecting you to digest it and integrate it successfully. They ignore the weak link in the chain—the trader.

- The examples, illustrations, and discussions are specific, clearly noted, and backed up with concise charts to bring the points home.

- While many other books promise to reveal how you can begin with a relatively small amount of capital, they often fall short in giving you specific tools. This book delivers them to you.

- The methods, techniques, and systems are innovative and creative. They will teach you a variety of approaches. You won't be doing the same thing that everyone else is doing. And this will, I believe, give you the edge that you need in order to make money at this game.

- Where possible, I provide you with statistics regarding the efficacy of each method or system. This does not guarantee the future; however, it will give you a clear and objective idea of how well the methods have worked in the past.

- And finally, I give you enough choices so that you can determine what interests you and where you stand your best chances of success as a day trader.

I hope you enjoy my book. But more than enjoyment, I hope it brings you profits. That's what this game is about. If I can clarify any of the concepts, methods, or indicators discussed herein, you can contact me via e-mail at jake@2chimps.com and I will reply to you as soon as I can. Understand that I will personally attempt to respond to every e-mail that I receive; however, this is not always possible. At times I will have an assistant respond to you. You may also visit my stock trading Web site at www.2chimps.com.

Jacob Bernstein

Acknowledgments

I would like to extend thanks to all the people who helped make this book possible. Although we have been out of touch for several decades, I thank John Rusin for giving me my first, and best, lessons in stocks.

And to my office staff, of course, I am always indebted since they make my work easier and more efficient. Nan Martin Barnum has agonized over this manuscript countless times, organizing, correcting, editing, cutting, pasting, and giving valuable suggestions such as, "Can't you make that more interesting?" or "Don't try to fill every page to its maximum." Marilyn Kinney, my office manager, deserves credit for her probing questions and expert proofreading. Her use of the dictionary in helping me find the right word at the right time has been invaluable. Patricia Lomax has worked wonders with my schedule, giving me much needed blocks of time to write. And Mary Kinney has been an excellent proofreader as well as a great help in keeping me on schedule.

Glen Larson of Genesis Financial Data was extremely helpful in providing me with stock tick data for system testing my trading methods and ideas, while Mark Shriver, also at Genesis Financial Data, was a major help in guiding me through the installation of the data and its manipulation in TradeStation™.

Larry Williams gets special thanks for allowing me to borrow from his rich storehouse of technical indicators and ideas as well as his unique approach to the markets.

The good people at Omega Research have produced an outstanding software product that allows traders to develop, back-test, and trade systems in real time. I also thank Omega for permission to reproduce charts and system reports from their TradeStation™ software.

CQG Inc. has also developed an exceptionally good software product that allows traders to track markets and technical indicators tick by tick. The use of their CQG for Windows product was a valuable help to me and I thank them for permission to use charts printed with their software.

Finally, no book would go to press were it not for the final edit and layout. Ginny Carroll at North Market Street Graphics was a pleasure to work with. She made the often agonizing task of editing and layout fast, easy, and perhaps even pleasurable.

The Compleat
Guide to Day
Trading Stocks

Introduction

... All round me walls are crumbling ...
horizons infinitely remote and incredibly
beautiful, stand revealed. It is as though
threads, previously unknown and unsuspected,
begin to reach out and bind things together ...
                              P. D. OUSPENSKY,
                    A New Model of the Universe

If you bought this book in search of the Holy Grail, then you bought the wrong book. Within these pages you will not find magical methods, get-rich-quick schemes, or infallible systems. If this is what you're looking for, there are plenty of other books, courses, seminars, and videotapes that promise to deliver the goods you're searching for. If you believe their claims, then you will be one more disappointed customer who was promised the world on a platter but ended up with a dog biscuit on the kennel floor.

The fact is that there are no magical methods or secret weapons for beating the markets. If you seek success as a day trader, you'll have to make your money the good old-fashioned way: you'll have to do some work. You'll have to earn it. You won't be able to earn it without effort, knowledge, experience, starting capital, patience, persistence, time, and one-half teaspoon of luck. But luck is by far the smallest component and least important aspect of the equation for success. The other considerations mentioned here are far more important.

The Fastest Game in Town

Day trading in stocks has become the biggest game in town. Growth in the day-trading business has been explosive. Almost daily we hear tales of traders who have achieved great wealth by their adventures in day trading. Hopeful investors come to the markets weekly by the thousands, eager to play the game, with the dream that they, too, will become independently wealthy. But in reality few succeed—not because the game is terribly difficult to learn, but rather because they fail to learn the game.

Ironically, these are primarily sensible people who in other aspects of their lives exercise good judgment, reason, and restraint. Many are not the typical risk takers that we see in a casino, at a racetrack, or buying $1000 worth of lottery tickets at the mini-mart. I'm talking about schoolteachers, doctors, dedicated blue-collar-worker fathers, housewives, taxi drivers, and secretaries. Fascination with the stock market as a national lottery—particularly with day trading as the way to achieve fast wealth—has helped create what I consider to be the most speculative market in history, with the exception perhaps of the indignity that ruled the Dutch tulip mania of the 1600s.

What never ceases to amaze me is that people who might otherwise be risk averse by their very nature or financial means enter the market as aspiring day traders and somehow, by some mysterious diabolical force, lose their sensibilities, their rationality, and their otherwise intelligent nature. They attempt to play a game they have not learned. They somehow think that they can emerge victorious against those who are professionals. And they delude themselves into believing that success is just a stone's throw away. Perhaps they have been led to the height of sophistry by what they have read in the newspapers or seen on television. Or perhaps they are driven by the growing need to compete in a society that is slowly but surely raising its standard of living.

I recently heard a shocking evening news report. New lawyers, fresh out of law school, have been able to land their first jobs at salaries in excess of $125,000 per year. I was flabbergasted. It's no wonder that middle-class Americans feel so pressured to compete—so pressured to acquire wealth. They see people all around them doing it, and, of course, they feel the need to compete as well. But the need is not all in their minds. The average American family of the late 1990s and early 2000s with two children can barely make ends meet on a combined salary of $50,000. It takes much more than that to successfully raise a family with today's standard of living.

And this is what, to a great extent, drives many traders to come to the markets. Those who can learn and follow a sensible and well-planned method of investing can do well—many have. Those who can learn and follow a well-planned and -implemented approach to day trading can also do well, yet I believe that winners are in the minority. You ask why? There are a number of essential reasons, all of which will be discussed in this book. But the primary reasons are threefold:

- *New day traders come to the markets with very limited capital.* They are knocked out of the game after a few losses. And for them, the game is over until they can amass a new amount of capital. Simply stated, they begin with too little money and this essentially limits severely their odds of success, since they are out of the game following a few losses.

- *New traders often lack the education they need in order to have a fighting chance at success.* They somehow believe that the game is simple and that skill is not a major factor. They learn the hard way that they are dead wrong.

- *New traders often lack discipline.* While they may have learned a few methods for successful day trading, they lack the ability to consistently apply the rules. And this is their downfall. Discipline is a function of experience. If experience is lacking, then discipline may also be in short supply.

Like Flying an Airplane Without Lessons

No sensible person would think about getting into the cockpit of an airplane and attempting to fly it without lessons. The result of trying to fly a plane without lessons would most certainly be a crash. Yes, some of those who attempt this feat of bravery or foolhardiness will succeed, but they are few and far between. Perhaps some of those who succeed will have read *The Complete Mindless Book of Flight Instruction* (a fictitious book, of course). They will have learned the basics and they will succeed. But this is highly unlikely. In all probability the result will be a disaster. This is what tends to happen to the individual who comes to the stock market as a day trader with a little money and virtually no education.

Perhaps such individuals have been further deluded into thinking that they will succeed by the growing trend toward *positive mental attitude* and self-help. Yes, I think that it's fantastic to have a positive attitude. But in order to achieve success and make positive attitudes work for you, you must begin with a minimal skill level. And, sadly, most day traders haven't the slightest idea of how to win at the game. We can tell so much from their vocabulary, from listening to them talk about what they plan to do. Do any of these statements sound familiar to you?

- *I think I'll take a shot at day trading.*
- *If Joe can make a ton of money day trading, so can I.*
- *I'd like to take a gamble on day trading stocks.*
- *I have a few thousand bucks to risk. Day trading stocks might be a good idea.*
- *Day trading is easy. People are making money at it every day.*
- *I'd rather gamble on the market than buy a lotto ticket.*

The road to success in day trading stocks is not so much a function of luck as it is a function of skill. While there are those who will be successful as a result of luck, the odds of profit as a result of luck are slim. You will be far better off getting some education first. And that is what this book is all about!

By way of introduction there are four broad categories of trading style in the current day-trading arenas. They are as follows.

The Specialist Approach

This method seeks to capture profits on very small moves (often $\frac{1}{16}$ of a point) using large blocks of shares (i.e., 1000 shares or more). The specialist approach is so named since it attempts to do what the market maker or specialist does. This method is simple and straightforward, and it can work if you learn it well and if you can actually buy the shares at your price.

A number of books discuss this popular method of day trading. While this approach has its assets, it is highly competitive and not nearly as successful as many would have you believe. The larger profits are made by day trading volatile stocks that make large moves within the day time frame.

Volatility Trading

This method is based on taking advantage of large intraday price moves in volatile stocks that have sufficient liquidity (i.e., trading volume) to allow for good order execution. The methods are purely technical and more often than not are computer based. The techniques I will teach you in this book are designed to capture such moves with a fairly high degree of reliability and accuracy.

"Guts" Trading

This is not a trading approach at all! Yet in spite of its lack of specificity and its gambling-type mentality, it's the method used by far too many traders. As its name implies, there is no consistent approach here. The day trader makes decisions based on a nonspecific, often emotion-laden, and subjective method.

Typically such approaches are destined to failure unless the individual is especially good at cutting losses and is extremely lucky. Of course, this approach would also be appropriate for those who are more than mildly clairvoyant.

Neural Networks

This is an up-and-coming approach to day trading that employs advanced computer hardware and software concepts that "learn" how to day trade based on various models of artificial intelligence. A great deal of work is now being done on these methods, yet the amount of published and viable research is sparse. Those who have been working with neural networks for a number of years are well aware of both their promise and their limitations at this time.

Why Day Trading in Stocks Has Become a Viable Venture (or Adventure)

In addition to the large price moves in the day time frame, several other factors have combined to create numerous profit opportunities for the stock day trader. Low commissions have significantly reduced the cost of active trading. Powerful computer technology at relatively low cost has facilitated the process of trading system research as well as online order entry. This confluence of circumstances has created a multitude of opportunities for all who seek to trade stocks within the day time frame.

What was once the domain of the professional stock trader has now become fair game for all traders who have the time, speculative capital, persistence, motivation, knowledge, and methodology to succeed in this high-stakes game. Too many day traders enter the stock market without the proper trading tools. They fail to use appropriate systems and methods or they trade "by the seat of their pants." They lose money and wonder why. *The Compleat Guide to Day Trading Stocks* is designed to educate stock day traders in techniques and systems that can help them generate maximum profits while minimizing risk. *The Compleat Guide to Day Trading Stocks* will guide novice and veteran stock day traders through the treacherous waters of day trading, as it teaches them to avoid questionable trading approaches while learning profitable methods.

Specific systems, methods, and timing indicators will be presented, along with their results. This book will also teach you the nuances of order placement, market entry and exit, broker selection, risk management, and portfolio diversification. Special attention will be given to day trading the high-priced technology sector stocks, with emphasis on capturing profits from intraday price swings.

If you have studied my methods you will be able to enter the highly competitive day-trading arena with an edge over your opponents. Your odds of success will be vastly greater than they are for those who come to the game with little knowledge, no knowledge, faulty knowledge, or erroneous knowledge. Yes, I do believe that the information in this book can help you. But it's up to you to be a good student and to work hard at learning the rules, methods, skills, and applications.

1

To Trade or Not to Trade

*Prosperity is not without many fears and
distastes.*   SIR FRANCIS BACON

We have all read about or heard about or know about someone who has "made a killing" day trading stocks. In today's highly volatile markets, stocks move up and down so rapidly, so often, with such large magnitude, that day-trading opportunities abound. To a certain extent, the day-trading arena has become a legalized gambling pit, sanctioned not only by government regulatory bodies but also by the "suits" of Wall Street.

Many traders have been forced into day trading simply to avoid the large equity swings in their stock portfolios. Yet the majority of traders are lured to the markets by the promise of quick profits, large profits, and easy profits. Numerous advertisements online, in newspapers, in magazines, on the radio, by e-mail, and via "snail mail" tout the potential of day trading.

Don't Assume Day Trading Is as Easy as You've Heard

This has given many of us the impression that day trading is somehow an easy venture and that all one need do is buy a computer, open an account, fund it, find a method of trading, apply it, and watch the profits roll in. If you are one of the people who believe the hype, then I offer a prayer for you to the gods of day trading since you are the proverbial sheep going to the slaughter. The decision to day trade is not one to be taken lightly or made without knowing the facts, the risks, and the potentials.

Before you flip past the pages in this chapter, seeking the meat in this book, I urge you to reconsider. You can read and give serious consideration at this time to the issues raised in this chapter, or you may find yourself coming back to read it after you have joined the legions who have lost money as a day trader. If my words seem stern or perhaps ominous, they are so by intent. I cannot possibly overstate the importance of the issues raised in this chapter.

Facts to Consider

The decision to day trade in stocks should not be made lightly or without full knowledge of the facts, both in favor of and opposed to this venture. While some of the facts in both categories are unique to the individuals in question and cannot be stated specifically due to their specificity to those individuals, the facts that are known can be stated and discussed.

Here are the pros and cons of day trading in stocks. In each of the following points I present both sides of the argument.

Day Trading in Stocks Can Be Very Profitable

Yes, this is true. Some individuals have been able to make a large amount of money day trading in stocks. Although it is true that not all individuals who day trade will make money, there is still the possibility that success can be achieved in this endeavor.

Yet the bad news is that the majority of people who attempt to day trade will not make money. In fact, they will lose money. There are many reasons for this. They will be discussed later in this book.

Only a Small Amount of Money Is Needed to Begin Day Trading

There are many who would have us believe that this is true. And to a certain extent, it is indeed the case. Yet what we are often not told is that the odds of success are closely correlated with the amount of starting capital. The more you begin with, the more likely your odds of success.

If your amount of starting capital is small, then you will be knocked out of the game after only a few losses. Yet if you begin with more money, you will have more chances to get the big trades when they come.

The Small Trader Can Compete with the Professional Trader Due to New Rules

There has been much hype about changes in the rules and regulations governing the execution of orders from the small trader. The Small Order Execution System (SOES) has given the average trader the same opportunity to get filled on orders at a fair price as is afforded to large traders (i.e., those with orders to buy a large number of shares).

This positive change has indeed made the small trader more competitive, yet it is not a panacea. It will not cure lack of discipline, lack of trading system or method, lack of self-control, or ignorance. As much as the SOES has helped improve prospects of success, the obstacles are still many. In the long run SOES will help you, but it will be of no value if other aspects of your day trading are either lacking or faulty.

Market Volatility Creates Many Day Trading Opportunities

Yes, this is true. Yes, it's also true that the more volatility there is within the day time frame, the more opportunities there will be to day trade. Yet, the mere presence or availability of an opportunity does not ipso facto ensure that the day trader will be successful.

Opportunities in today's markets abound, but unfortunately, so do undisciplined, inexperienced, and ineffective traders.

Successful Day Trading Requires a Commitment

Too many newcomers to the day-trading game are not aware of either the time or the commitment required for success. Some have been misled into thinking that success is as simple as opening an account. Others view day trading as an open treasure chest whose riches need merely be plucked. Both views are incorrect.

Time, experience, effort, commitment, consistency, persistence, money, and skill are all necessary components that lead to profitable day trading. Day trading is a business. It is not a sure thing. And it is not something that everyone can do. The good news is that success is possible.

The bad news is that it requires effort. If you enter the game either unaware of the requirements or unwilling to meet them, then you will most likely fail unless you are extremely lucky. I have seen too many individuals who are otherwise successful in their own professions or businesses fail at day trading simply because they refuse to treat day trading as a business.

It's a sad irony. They know what it takes to be a success in their own businesses, yet they cannot apply the same discipline to day trading.

Live Quotes or Not?

Another important consideration in determining whether you want to be a day trader is the need for live quotes. While live quotes can be obtained online, often at no charge from your broker, the ability to analyze prices, either in the form of charts with timing indicators or in the form of trading systems, often requires additional software.

The cost of this software can be as high as several thousand dollars. And the cost of updating your data, either on a tick-by-tick basis or at the end of the day, adds to the fixed costs of doing business. Add to this the cost of a computer and you have an initial outlay that could easily run to $5000.

To many day traders this is unacceptable. Yet, in some cases, to begin trading with a less sophisticated setup may limit your chances for success. You are better off knowing this before you make your decision to day trade than to begin day trading only to find out that you started your venture (or adventure) without the necessary equipment.

If You Currently Have a Full-Time Job

If you currently have a full-time job other than trading, then please read this section. If you do not have a job at this time and plan to make day trading your full-time job or if you have a full-time job and plan to quit in order to day trade, then skip this section and read the next one.

Many aspiring day traders attempt to play the game while at the same time keeping their day jobs. This may not sit well with your boss. I advise you against taking the risk of losing your job.

If you are self-employed, then it is certainly possible to day trade and do your job at the same time. In this case you will need to select a trading system or method that is compatible with your work schedule. It will not be possible for you to trade a method that requires you to watch price quotes the entire day.

If you are not self-employed, note that there are several methods in this book which are not as attention intensive. They will allow you to place orders before the trading day begins or at the end of the trading day for the next day's trading session. No matter which methods or systems you select, please take into consideration the realistic requirements of your job, whether you are self-employed or work for someone else.

If You Do Not Have a Full-Time Job

If you do not now have a full-time job, then I will assume that you are financially independent. If you do not have a full-time job and if you intend to day trade with money that you need for living expenses and so forth, then I suggest you not day trade the markets.

Not only is it unsound financial management to trade with money you and/or your family may need for the purpose of living expenses, but to do so would also add pressure to your trading.

2
Let the Game Begin

The only limit to our realization of tomorrow
will be our doubts of today.
FRANKLIN D. ROOSEVELT

A Brief History of Day Trading in Stocks

The longest lasting and largest bull market in the history of U.S. stocks started in 1982. Since then the Dow Jones Industrial Average has risen from a low of 769 to a recent high of 11,568. And as of this writing, the major bull trend continues. Trading volume has also increased from a few hundred thousand shares daily to about 1 billion shares daily in the Dow Jones Industrials, and trading volume in the NASDAQ has soared as well.

As trading volume and liquidity have grown, so has participation in the markets by investors from all walks of life. While it is true that institutions such as mutual funds, insurance companies, banks, and pension funds are the primary forces in this market, the independent, individual trader has also become an important player.

As share prices have increased, often to extremely high levels, the dollar-per-share movement in stocks has also increased. A 5 percent move in a stock at $40 per share is a $2 move, whereas a 5 percent move in a $300 stock is $15. At 100 shares, this means a $1500 move intraday as opposed to a $200 move intraday. The difference is substantial.

And it is precisely this difference that has been a significant factor in creating day-trading opportunities. But opportunity is only one side of the risk/reward coin. The potential for loss has also been a factor in the growth of day trading. How is that so? The answer is simple. Given the large price swings that can often occur overnight, some traders have found it safer to exit their trades at the end of the day session.

Preliminaries: Defining a Few Terms

Before digging too deeply into the technical aspects of stock day trading, we'll need to attend to a few housekeeping details that pertain to our task. First among these is a brief but necessary definition of terms. Let's take a look at some important terminology that will be used throughout this book. While many of these terms are given cursory definitions in the glossary located at the end of this book, the definitions in this chapter are more extensive and precise.

If you are familiar with them, feel free to skip over this section. However, if you are not well-versed in their meanings, then I suggest you read the following carefully. Although you may think that this is an unnecessary waste of time and space, I cannot tell you how surprised I am at the all-too-common lack of knowledge most individuals have about *trading* in general and *day trading* in particular—what it is and what it is designed to achieve.

Bid/Offer

As simple as these terms may be, there are still many investors and traders who fail to understand their meaning. A *bid* is an order to *buy* at a given price, whereas an *offer* is an order to *sell* at a given price. *Buyers bid* for a given stock, while *sellers offer* a given stock. This is in no way different from what you would see at an auction.

The auctioneer stands at the podium, *offering* merchandise or goods that have been placed up for *sale*. The buyers make *bids* to buy the given items at a certain price. If a stock is at 45 and I want to buy 100 shares (henceforth the abbreviation used for this will be 100S) at 43, I would place an order to buy 100S @ 43. This would constitute a *bid* at 43. If I wanted to sell 100S @ 47 this would be an *offer* at 47.

Day Trade

A day trade is a trade that is entered and exited on the same day. It does not mean that the trade will be held overnight, that it will be kept overnight if profitable, that it will always be entered on the opening and exited on the close, or that it will not entail risk. It is important to remember that, by definition, *day trades are always over by the end of the trading day.* A day trade is no longer a day trade if it is held through to the next trading session.

Day traders will not hold positions to the next trading session, regardless of how they have fared during the day. This means that a loss is a loss and a profit is a profit and that all scores are settled by the end of the trading session—win, lose, or draw. Day trades may be entered at any time during the day, but they must be closed out by the end of the day.

Day Trader

A trader who day trades is called a *day trader.* A day trader is not an investor. A day trade is not an investment. *A day trade is a speculation and day traders are speculators.*

Whether they do so in stocks, options, futures, mutual funds, currencies, or any other vehicle, a day trade is merely a speculative activity designed to capitalize on intraday price swings. The swings can be large or small. The day trader can use a variety of techniques, systems, methods, and/or trading systems to achieve his or her goals.

Intermediate-Term Trading

An intermediate-term trade is one usually held for several months. Many traders, money managers, and investors prefer such trades. This is certainly a lower-pressure way to make money in the stock market. And in the long run, it is likely to be more profitable than day trading. However, it does not suit either the temperament or the pocketbook of many investors or traders.

Simply stated, in order to make good money in stocks over the intermediate term and the long term, you need to begin with a fairly large amount of money. Intermediate-term traders seek to take advantage of larger price swings but do not wish to hold stocks for several years or more. They seek to maximize their capital by holding stocks for larger moves over a period of months, thereby attempting to capitalize on large market swings.

The day trader, on the other hand, seeks to make the best use of his or her capital by investing and reinvesting it daily in order to build account equity (i.e., profits).

Investing

A stock market investor can hold positions for several years or as long as several decades. What the day trader does is the complete antithesis of what the investor does, but with one exception. They both try to make money, but they approach the task in distinctly different ways and with markedly different methods.

The motivations that lead investors to day trade, short-term trade, or intermediate-term trade differ from one individual to another and are numerous and complex. They are not merely a matter of available investment capital, but they are also intricately related to age, perception, temperament, trading methodology, and perhaps even the sex of the investor (i.e., there are probably more male day traders than female day traders, but this gap appears to be closing rapidly).

Market Entry and Exit

Market entry means simply to establish a new long or short position. Market exit means to close out an existing long or short position. There are several different types of orders that may be used for entering and exiting markets. These will be discussed later.

The type of order you use to enter or exit a day-trade position is important since the commission can be different for different types of orders and certain types of orders should only be used in certain situations.

Optimization, Curve Fitting

The procedure one uses to create a trading system that is based on historical data is called *optimizing. When a trading system developer optimizes a system, he or she does so in order to generate a set of system rules that have performed well on historical data.* Although the system appears to have worked well in the past, it is in fact fitted to the data.

The given system can be optimized in a number of different ways. Depending upon the method used to optimize a system, the results will have varying degrees of success in their ability to be replicated in the future.

If a system is optimized using realistic criteria (loose optimization), then the results could likely be replicated in the future on data the system has not used in its historical test. However, if the system developer uses highly specific criteria (tight optimization), then the results will look good for past data but the odds of the system working in the future will be slim.

A tightly optimized or curve-fitted system will rarely perform well in the future. To a given extent, most system testing involves some degree of optimization or curve fitting. Opinions on curve fitting differ sharply among market experts. I will discuss this topic in greater detail later.

Position Trader, Position Trading, Investor

As I have stated previously, a day trader is one who day trades. As soon as a day trader holds a position overnight, he or she cannot refer to the trade as a day trade or to him or herself as a day trader. *A position trader, however, holds trades for an extended period.* The position trader is also called an *investor*.

While there is no stigma associated with being an investor in stocks, being a day trader in stocks carries with it a certain image or stereotype. This will be discussed later. Although I do not believe that there is anything wrong with being a day trader, you must be careful what you tell yourself about your goals as a day trader, or you may begin to believe things that are not necessarily true.

A day trader is committed to a certain specific course of action. That course of action is to buy stocks and to sell them within the time of a day. This means that the day trader will be out before the closing bell. To exit in the aftermarket is not what I consider day trading. To exit on the opening of the next day is not day trading. In fact, it defeats the entire principle of day trading.

To sway from this course of action is to subvert the intent of day trading in stocks. To stray from the day-trading objective is to abandon its principles and to acquire a new set of expectations that may not be consistent with your original objectives.

I urge you, therefore, to be committed to your course of action once you have determined it. The day trader can also be an investor; however, I believe that the methods of selecting stocks, as well as the goals, are distinctly different and not mutually compatible. If you want to be an investor, then do yourself a service and do not refer to yourself as a day trader, lest you confuse your goals.

Simply stated, what's right for the investor is not necessarily right for the day trader, and vice versa. Investors are often willing—and often required—to hold a losing position for quite some time in the expectation that it will eventually become profitable. To the day trader, this is a violation of the most sacred and essential rule of day trading.

Is it possible for traders to wear different hats at different times or many hats at the same time? Yes! There is nothing wrong with trading in different time frames at the same time, provided you do so with specific structure and follow objective rules that will be explained later in this book.

But, remember, this book is primarily—in fact, exclusively—for the stock day trader and not for the investor. Investors are advised to find information on their goals in other books. There are many outstanding books on investing. The book you are currently reading is an outstanding book on day trading.

Short-Term Trading, Short-Term Trader

A short-term trader, as opposed to a day trader or an investor, is one who trades for relatively short-term market swings of from 2 to 10 days' duration. There is no firm definition of the exact length of time short-term traders hold their positions.

The distinction between a short-term trader and an investor is not as precise as is the distinction between a day trader and all other types of traders. A day trader trades within the day time frame as a firm rule, whereas investors and short-term traders' time lengths are not as specifically defined.

Some of the techniques described in this book may be applied to short-term trading as well as day trading in stocks. In fact, I will give you a few methods for short-term stock trading in order to demonstrate one cogent and irrevocable fact: *while day trading has its advantages, short-term trading is potentially more lucrative since it gives the stocks you're trading more time to make bigger moves.*

Bear in mind, however, that the short-term methods I recommend are not to be used in their given form for investing. Investing is a distinctly different topic with numerous possible methods and many different philosophies.

Slippage

Slippage is the tendency for day trades to get a poor price execution on a market order. If a stock is dropping or rising quickly and you place an "at the market" order, you may get a poor price execution even though your order may be filled within seconds.

While this is less of a problem in day trading stocks than it is in commodity futures or options, it is still a significant concern to the day trader who is trading a large number of shares in order to capitalize on very small moves. The slippage in buying and in selling a stock at the market can be large enough to totally offset the profits from such types of trading methods (more about this later).

Hence, when I refer to a given dollar or point amount deduction for slippage, I mean that I am deducting the given amount from every trade in a hypothetical back-test in order to represent more accurately what might have happened (more about this later).

A stock that tends to have too much slippage is, therefore, a stock for which quick and sudden price moves tend to result in price fills that are unexpectedly or unreasonably worse than what you expected. There are several ways in which to minimize slippage. These will also be discussed in later chapters.

Specialist/Market Maker

A specialist or market maker is the individual or firm that handles the shares of stock in a given market or markets on the floor of the exchange or via an electronic exchange. The specialist maintains an inventory of shares in a stock or stocks in order to facilitate a liquid or functional market. The specialist makes money by buying and selling large amounts of stock at small profits.

Some of the day-trading methods that have become popular in recent years compete with the specialist inasmuch as they attempt to trade large blocks of shares for small moves. In some cases, depending upon the commission a day trader pays, profits can be made on moves as small as ¼ point.

Timing Indicators, Timing Signals

A timing indicator is defined as any specific technique, whether fundamental or technical, which objectively indicates market entry, market exit, or the underlying condition (i.e., bullish, bearish, neutral) of a given stock or market index. A timing indicator can also be called a *timing signal.* I will use the terms interchangeably in this book.

The working definition given here is intentionally general for the specific purposes of this book. You will find, in later chapters, that there are literally hundreds of timing indicators. Timing indicators must be objective—that is, not subject to interpretation. An indicator which is subject to interpretation is not an indicator; it is, rather, a technique and, therefore, subject to different interpretations by different traders and even by the same trader in different situations.

I will make every effort in this book to differentiate between timing indicators, trading techniques, and trading methods. As you will see, however, my focus will be primarily on timing indicators and systems.

Trading Systems

A trading system, as opposed to a trading method, timing indicator, trading technique, market pattern, and so on, is an organized methodology containing specific entry and exit indicators. The given indicators will signal specific buy, sell, or stay-out advice to the stock day trader.

Additionally, the trading system has an operational set of procedures (called *rules*) including, but not limited to, various risk management (follow-up *stop-loss rules*) methods, and techniques. A trading system is implemented by following specific timing signals that dictate market entry and exit either at buy or sell stop levels or at the market.

I am defining this term specifically here in order to distinguish a trading system from other market techniques which are not as specific and/or which do not follow a predetermined set of procedures. We find that stock day traders tend not to follow systems but are, rather, seat-of-the-pants traders who use a combination of indicators, "gut feel" (intuition), and other seemingly objective analytical techniques.

Trading systems, by their very definition, must necessarily be operational and somewhat rigid in their construction for the purpose of delineating specific procedures which, theoretically, should lead to profitable trading, provided the system is functioning as intended or tested.

As previously noted (and will again be noted in various other locations throughout this book), most traders do not follow a trading system. They delude themselves into thinking that they are trading according to a system or plan; however, they violate the rules of their trading system so frequently that we cannot define their actions as systematic. This definition is designed to set the stage for more extensive commentary on the subject in a later chapter.

I reiterate also that a trading system must be systematic or it is not a trading system, regardless of what the individual who professes to be trading a "system" may think. The vast majority of traders begin with a system but alter it to suit their internal feelings about the markets to the extent that they are not following a system at all (other than, perhaps, in their own minds).

While I believe that a trading system or, at the very minimum, a highly specific trading method is necessary for success as a stock day trader, there are those who succeed without a system or method. Although profitable day trading in stocks is certainly possible without a system, I believe that having a system increases the odds of success by imposing structure on your trading behavior as well as a set of defined parameters that may be intrinsic to market behavior.

In addition, a trading system can help improve trader discipline by decreasing or eliminating the tendency for impulsive decisions (to which virtually all traders fall victim at one time or another).

Trading Technique

A trading technique, as opposed to a timing indicator, timing signal, or trading system, is a fairly loose collection of procedures which assists traders in making decisions about buying, selling, or holding a stock. Frequently a trading technique consists of one or more timing indicators combined with general entry and exit rules and/or risk management procedures.

A trading technique is, therefore, not a trading system but rather an approach to trading which is generally objective but not nearly as precise or rigid as is a trading system. As a result, trading techniques tend to leave too much room for interpretation and, therefore, they are not as objective as timing signals or trading systems.

Any approach to trading that leaves room for interpretation is a potential victim of bias, emotion, and undisciplined trading. And these are often the downfall of day traders, short-term traders, and investors.

These, then, are some of the terms that I will use throughout the course of this book. Terms not noted herein will be defined as they are introduced. Please note that my intent in redefining terms that you may already know is not to insult your intelligence but rather to make absolutely certain that we are communicating, since this is of paramount importance when teaching specific trading systems, techniques, and methods. Furthermore, many terms commonly used nowadays are not clearly understood by the individuals using them.

The Lure of Day Trading

My recent search of the term *day trading* on the Internet produced 3,112,347 matches. A similar search conducted only a few years ago would have returned only a handful of matches. What is it about day trading that has attracted so many new (and totally inexperienced) traders since the mid-1990s? What do they expect? And above all, what makes them think they can be successful at this high-stakes, hard-hitting game?

Clearly, the attraction of day trading stems from the fact that daily trading ranges have been very large, particularly in the high-flying Internet stock sector. This has created potentially large profit opportunities for day traders. More accurately, however, I should say that this has created the *perception* of profit potential. In fact, there are not many traders who will be able to capitalize on such moves, for various and sundry reasons that will be discussed later in this book.

While the large intraday price swings have created the possibility of profit, yet another reason for the growth in popularity of day trading in stocks is the introduction of SOES (Small Order Execution System). In effect, this system gives the small, off-the-floor trader an advantage in getting orders filled at fair prices. The competitive edge of the professional trader has been diminished, thus allowing the public a more reasonable chance at success in short-term and day trading.

In addition to the preceding, the cost of commissions for those who are willing to maintain large account balances at brokers is no longer a serious factor in the quest for success as a speculator. Large blocks of stock can be traded for the same price as small blocks of stock. Hence, a day trader can trade numerous times a day without paying a prohibitively large portion of his or her profits to the brokerage firm. The cost of commissions, although still an important consideration, is no longer a barrier to profitable trading.

Still another factor that has added to the allure of day trading is the availability of real-time price quotations and sophisticated computer systems that are designed to provide instant information and technical analysis to the trader. Often the quotes and analysis programs are available free of charge to day traders who maintain sufficiently large account balances or who trade actively. Without the cost of live data and computers, yet another cost of doing business has been eliminated as an impediment to the day trader's success.

Finally, the ability to enter orders electronically and to secure virtually immediate price executions on market orders without having to call a broker has been one of the greatest factors behind the popularity and tremendous growth of day trading since the mid-1990s. Yet, as stated, none of the facilitating factors cited herein are guarantees of success. They are merely tools that may make success more probable. They are by no means guarantees or recipes for profits. This is an important fact that many aspiring day traders have discovered. And some have learned this lesson the painful way by losing considerable amounts of money.

The Realities of Day Trading in Stocks

With all of the aforementioned advantages for the day trader, what are the possible limiting factors or risks? Clearly, the risk is that of losing money. Moreover, most people who attempt day trading know very little about the markets, about day-trading techniques, or about what can happen when markets move against them quickly. Many novice day traders are only accustomed to stocks like Amazon.com rallying $24 on bullish news, whereas they have not experienced the behavior of stocks in extended bear markets.

In fact, most traders don't even sell stocks short. Therefore, when stocks decline sharply and quickly, many day traders who are long stocks are taken by surprise as the bearish storm develops around them. All too often they freeze, unable to take action due to their lack of experience. By the time they close out their losing trade(s), the loss is much larger than it would have been had they exited their trade early on.

Still another danger—one that you may find either improbable or even laughable—is that of addiction. Some day traders approach the markets as a legalized form of gambling, sanctioned by government, society, and the financial world. They are gamblers at heart and they approach the day-trading game from the perspective of the gambler. Some individuals who may have a latent addictive personality may find themselves hooked on day trading, whether their foray makes them money or not. I believe that this is a danger far more insidious and far less obvious than most people believe. Yet if the markets continue to facilitate day trading, we will hear more about the addicted trader, and we will recognize the dangers.

In addition to these realities of day trading is the fact that, all too often, day traders tend to lose their longer-term perspective. By focusing on immediate results, immediate profits, immediate feedback, virtually instant price executions, and ultra-quick trading, the long-range view is obscured. And this can hurt the individual who ignores the longer term in order to devote full attention to day trading. The well-rounded trader will maintain a balanced portfolio consisting of diversified investments—some shorter-term, some intermediate-term, and some long-term. Should the day-trading results be negative, there will still be other investments to fall back on.

Stress is still another reality of the day-trading world. When dealing with large sums of money (relative to the trader, of course), tensions can run high, losses can hurt more than mere emotions, and profits can cause extreme highs. Mood swings are common in many day traders, while stress runs high. We are all aware of the long-term debilitating effects of stress on human physiology and the immune system. Not too many day traders are capable of coping effectively with the stress of day trading. Among such individuals, a variety of psychological, physiological, and psychophysio-logical difficulties may occur as a direct result of day trading.

The bottom line here is simple. If day trading is so severely stressful to you that you act out your frustrations on family or friends, then the price you pay for your success is too high. If you find yourself kicking the cat or dog—or worse, abusing your spouse or children—then day trading is not for you.

Day Trading in Stocks as an Offshoot of Day Trading in Futures

As I noted earlier in this book, day trading is not a new phenomenon to the financial markets. The preeminent day-trading markets are in futures.

Explosive growth in Treasury bond, currency, grain, petroleum, and stock index futures helped set the stage for the expansive movement in stock day trading. But I find that day trading in stocks is a far easier task than is day trading in futures.

With the leverage so high in futures (i.e., 1 to 3 percent margin) as compared to stocks, price moves are often violent, rarely giving the trader sufficient time to execute an order. Frequently, price executions, whether on market orders or limit orders, are very poor in such volatile and fast-moving markets. Consequently, it is extremely difficult for the general public to make money day trading in futures.

Although I believe that there are many techniques for profitably trading futures, I also believe that few people have the discipline to employ these methods. Stocks tend to move more slowly, tend to be more forgiving, and often give the trader more chances to make money. Yet the returns in stock day trading are often less spectacular than they can be in futures unless one is trading with a large amount of capital.

A futures day trader can begin with as little as $10,000 and have a chance at making big money. In stocks, a $10,000 account, even on margin, won't take you very far since you will be limited in the number of stocks and the number of shares you can trade. I will relate more about this later in the book.

How S&P 500 Futures Helped Create the Stock Day-Trading Frenzy

Until the introduction of S&P 500 futures trading in 1982, the world of futures trading was looked upon as the black sheep of the investment world. In fact, futures trading wasn't considered an investment; rather, it was considered to be the ultimate speculation. Conservative investors, sensible money managers, and rational traders were often discouraged from entering the commodity markets. Yet the markets continued to grow, their dollar aggregate trading often outpacing that of stocks.

Destabilizing economic forces and factors in the 1970s and 1980s resulted in heavy trading volume, both in Treasury bond futures and currency futures. Slowly but surely, domestic and foreign banks entered the futures markets in order to use them as a hedge against currency risk. Realizing the vital economic role that futures trading played in a capitalist society, the Chicago Mercantile Exchange, through its International Monetary Mart, introduced the S&P 500 futures contract as a new type of vehicle to facilitate the transfer of risk.

At first the market was looked on askance and approached with trepidation and suspicion by traditional commodity traders and stock investors. However, as the full realization of its potential uses spread, S&P 500 futures trading increased dramatically. This unique hybrid product bridged the gap between commodities and stocks. And upon the heels of S&P, there followed such futures markets as the Value Line, NYFE Index, FTSE-100 (London Stock Index), DAX (German Stock Index), CAC-40 (Paris Stock Index), NASDAQ, Russell 2000, Nikkei, Dow Jones, and a host of stock index futures the world over. In the year 2000, stock index futures are among the most actively traded of all futures contracts and now occupy a position of respect and functionality.

Day traders in traditional futures markets began to trade S&P futures. Stock traders and investors crossed over to the futures arena. And then, as the stock markets heated up the world over in the 1990s, futures traders crossed over into stocks and began day trading in a new venue.

Many futures day traders, including this writer, were intrigued by the stock day-trading game. It was a peculiar game compared to futures trading. It had many similar rules but a few significant differences. It was the same, but it was not the same. It was very much like the futures markets were in the late 1960s and early 1970s—a vast, generally uncharted land of opportunity, ripe for the picking!

Why the Day-Trading Game Continues

Some observers of market behavior have asserted that the stock market at the start of the millennium is a "national lottery." To a given extent, I agree with them. Today, stocks of some Internet-related companies that have no earnings (and are operating at significant deficits) are selling at twice, three times, or even seven times the price of many established blue-chip companies that have excellent earnings as well as dividends.

Based on initial public offerings (IPOs), hundreds of new millionaires, as well as a fairly large number of new billionaires, have been created in a matter of several years. Selling shares to the public is what has made them their money. As you well know, the stocks of many Internet-related ventures have soared. And this has helped keep the day-trading game going.

Should this technology boom end, other industries may become favorites and their stocks will be traded actively by day traders. In short, I believe that the day-trading game in stocks is here to stay. The only thing that may inhibit it is a severe and sustained stock market decline.

Yesterday and Today

Interest in the stock market and day trading has been further stimulated by a rash of books in the late 1990s, each more optimistic than the other. Among the top-selling books on the stock market, you'll find the following titles:

DOW 36,000: The New Strategy for Profiting from the Coming Rise in the Stock Market (James K. Glassman and Kevin A. Hasset, Times Books, 1999)

DOW 40,000: Strategies for Profiting from the Greatest Bull Market in History (David Elias, McGraw-Hill, 1999)

DOW 100,000: Fact or Fiction (Charles W. Kadiec and Ralph J. Acampora, Prentice Hall, 1999)

While these forecasts may all be right or wrong, the fact remains that public interest in stock trading is at an all-time high. Record trading volume and a rash of initial public offerings, a surge of stock splits, and relatively low interest rates (which facilitate margin trading) all help ensure continued interest in stocks, investing, and day trading.

A Basic Overview of Day-Trading Goals and Objectives

As the new millennium begins, the day-trading game is in high gear. Liquidity in most day-trading stocks is high and opportunities abound. The methods, systems, and techniques for trading are available. Commissions and margin interest are low. The speed of order execution is fast. Volatility is pervasive.

What more could a prospective or current day trader want or need in order to facilitate success? Simply stated, all of these assets are worthless unless the day trader has developed several prerequisite tools. They are as follows:

- A set of behaviors and/or rules that will facilitate implementation of the systems or methods, including market entry and exit, method of system implementation, and system updates.

- Risk management procedures, including stop loss, amount of capital being traded, and contingency plans to deal with unforeseen market events.

- Backup systems for order entry in the event online communications fail.

- Computer backup procedures if a computer is being used to track markets, perform research, and enter orders.
- A method or system to monitor performance of trading methods and systems in order to know at any given moment whether they are performing as expected or otherwise. A simple determination of the bottom-line dollar amount is insufficient and often fails to reveal potentially useful and significant details about system performance.

In addition to these, the day trader must have clear awareness of his or her goals, not only in terms of trading methodology but in terms of daily profit targets, whether in dollar amount, percentage accuracy, or a combination of performance variables.

Finally, the day trader must also have a procedure or method for continued research and development of his or her trading approach and or new systems or methods that become available.

An Overview of Day-Trading Mechanics

The mechanics of day trading are simple indeed. While individual methods, systems, and techniques can vary considerably, the mechanics are essentially similar no matter what method you use for selecting your day trades. Here is an overview of the mechanics:

Selection Methodology

This portion of the mechanical requirements can consist of either a computerized trading system, a methodology, a technique, or a combination of these. Some traders will select their trades on the basis of intuition (not necessarily an effective approach unless you're a bona fide psychic), while others will use highly sophisticated computer-generated systems.

Regardless of your method, whether computer based, gut feel, astrological, chart based, or derived from an advisory service or tip sheet, you will need to have a methodology. This is the first requirement.

Account

Although it goes without saying, you will need an account with sufficient funds. The amount you have in your account is a matter of personal preference, financial ability, goals, willingness to accept risk, available risk capital, and so on.

There is no hard-and-fast rule other than the fact that those who begin with smaller amounts tend to get knocked out of the game quickly since they do not have sufficient capital to withstand a series of losses.

Method of Order Entry

The choices here are simple. Either you will deal directly with a broker or brokers, or you will enter orders online via the computer. Of the two methods, the lowest-cost and often fastest way to get the order done is via electronic order entry.

Once you have decided on which approach you want to use, you'll need to decide on a brokerage firm. Do not make your decision on the basis of cost alone! The most important considerations for a serious day trader are speed of order execution and accessibility. If it takes too long to get your order filled or if it takes too long to log into your broker's location, then you will lose valuable time. And time is money for day traders.

Record-Keeping System

You'll need a method by which you can keep track of your trades. Your online broker often does this. You can access your account at any time to see your open positions, resting orders, account balances, and so on. Some also offer real-time tick-by-tick updating of positions and equity.

As an alternative, you can use some of the available features of various trading software programs such as the Omega Research ProSuite Radar Screen.™

Location

You will need a location from which to trade. While this is another obvious requirement, you have some choices. Essentially there are three choices.

You can trade either from your home or from a home office. Some traders conduct business from their boat, others from the comfort of their desk at home. Recently I saw a television report about a New York taxi driver who day trades from his vehicle. Either of the two—a home office or a business office—is acceptable as long as it gets the job done.

Your third choice is to trade from a brokerage firm or a day-trading office specifically set up for this purpose. The good news in such situations is that the costs are either minimal or the service is provided for free, and you can get state-of-the-art computerized trading approaches and analytical techniques as well as rapid price quotes. The bad news is that you may find yourself distracted by other traders.

Data Access

If you trade from your home or business office, then you will need to have access to real-time stock data (in most cases). Some day traders do not use live data in their methods. Some of these methods will be discussed in later chapters.

Most traders, however, will need and want real-time updates of stock prices. Others will attempt to get by with lower-cost delayed quotations and still others will attempt to get their prices from the television screen by watching the delayed price tickers on various business television programs.

My suggestion here is to do what works for you. But, remember, cheap does not necessarily translate into dollars when it comes to day trading (or most things in life). The vast majority of effective day-trading methods require online, tick-by-tick data delivered to you at the highest possible speed and accuracy.

Data Line

Once you have decided that you want or need live data, you'll need to decide on how you want the data delivered. There are numerous options, all a function of speed and cost. The faster the speed of delivery, the higher the cost.

The traditional modem for online access is rapidly disappearing as more efficient and faster delivery methods become available. Whether you decide to get your data via cable, modem, T1 line, or otherwise, consider your options. As noted, speed is of the essence for most day traders.

As you can see, the mechanical requirements are simple enough, but there are a number of choices you must make. Consider your choices carefully before you begin so that you won't end up with a "Rube Goldberg" combination.

Advanced Computer Hardware and Software Technology

Day trading is all about getting the edge—that small advantage over other day traders and market markers. There are many ways in which the edge can be obtained; however, it takes work, persistence, an effective trading approach, discipline, and consistency.

While you can get the edge without using a computer, I assure you that it is much easier to win at this game if you use a computer and the powerful software that is currently available. You'll gain the edge more often and with greater success. Note that this *does not mean* you'll need a computer in order to be successful. But it will help.

Most of the methods and systems described in this book require the use of a computer. And if you're going to use a computer, then you might as well get one that has plenty of memory, lots of hard-drive space, good graphics, and a fast processor.

Electronic Trading and Its Influence on Day Trading

Online or electronic trading is the current state of the art. Speed of trading and data delivery will continue to improve until virtually all traders who have access to current technology will have the same opportunities for trading and market analysis. The net effect of electronic trading has been and will continue to be an increase in the number of day traders, the amount of day trading, and day-trading opportunities. A recent news report indicated that the average time length which traders hold their stocks has decreased considerably in recent years.

The focus of many investors is shifting to short term. And this is understandable, since the markets are more volatile and liquid than ever before. Where such opportunities exist, opportunists step in to capitalize on them. The day trader is the quintessential opportunist. We can, therefore, expect electronic trading to result in a further expansion of day trading.

Yet remember above all that where there exists the opportunity for profit there is also the risk of loss. The yin and yang of day trading are forever in balance. It is your job as a day trader to step into the market when an imbalance exists and to capitalize on the temporary imbalance before conditions return to an equilibrium.

How Commission Costs Have Affected Day Trading

One of the factors limiting trader success in day trading was, for many years, the cost of commissions. However, since the advent of discount commissions it has become possible for day traders to overcome this limiting factor. As a result, more day traders than ever before have entered the day-trading game. As you may know, the brokerage business is highly competitive. It is now possible for active day traders to trade up to 5000 shares of a stock for a fixed commission. This makes the game more active and more viable. This trend is likely to continue.

The Internet as a Tool for Day Traders

The Internet has also helped increase virtually every aspect of day trading. Traders can get price quotes, data, market reports, and order executions quickly and at low cost. As Internet data transmission speed and bandwidth increase, the transfer of data will become faster and more efficient. And this will help the day trader considerably.

Order executions will become faster and this will help the online day trader. The Internet is rapidly becoming an indispensable tool for the day trader. If you are not yet connected to the Internet, then I recommend you get current with the technology. Sooner or later you will need to get connected. You might as well do it now. It will help you considerably.

The Future of Day Trading in Stocks

Day trading in stocks is here to stay. Unless trading volume in stocks narrows dramatically, day trading will continue to grow. I suspect that the length of time for holding stocks will continue to decline as the markets become more active and as intraday trading ranges expand. While it is not imperative that all investors become day traders, I suspect that those who learn how to day trade will be able to profit handsomely in the years ahead, as markets expand.

In addition to day trading in the U.S. markets, stock markets all over the world will become more active and day trading will grow substantially with the expansion of these markets. Day trading will continue to grow, not only in volume of shares traded but also in the stocks that can be day traded. I believe that every unit of effort you put into learning how to day trade will be an asset to you in the years ahead.

As long as you have the discipline, patience, and persistence to implement your knowledge, you will be glad you learned how to day trade. Just remember that unrealistic expectations will work against you as a day trader. Maintain a sensible and rational approach to your trading and you will do well.

The Next Step

Now that we've taken care of the overview and a few housekeeping details, we are ready to go on to the essence of day trading. In reading what follows I urge you to take your time. Don't plunge into day trading using only a portion of the information contained in this book. Take your time. Take notes. Evaluate my methods and systems. Determine whether they fit your needs.

You may find that some of the methods appeal to you more than others. You may find that some just don't strike you as enjoyable or perhaps as capable of being implemented, given your unique situation. Regardless, don't rush into trading after reading just a few pages of this book or after learning just a few ideas. Take the time to apply the ideas on paper before you use them.

Summary

Day trading has its assets, liabilities, systems, methods, procedures, requirements, profits, and potential losses. In order to effectively day trade, you will need to have a plan, the right tools, the right attitudes, a reasonable amount of starting capital, and a system or method. Organization, self-discipline, and experience will be your greatest assets.

Day trading is likely to grow rapidly in the years ahead. If you learn the skills, they should serve you well in the future. But learning the skills alone will not suffice. You need to implement your trades with consistency, objectivity, and accuracy.

3

Big Movers,
Big Winners, Big Losers

It takes a great deal of boldness and a great deal
of caution to make a great fortune . . . it
requires ten times as much wit to keep it.
RALPH WALDO EMERSON

The stock market of the new millennium is characterized by immense volatility. Huge moves occur not only on an overnight basis but intraday as well. While the potential for profit is seductive, in reality few traders will benefit from these dynamic moves. This chapter will explore some of the reasons, while introducing you to some basis strategies.

Who Benefits and Who Loses from Large Moves in Stocks?

What constitutes a big move in a stock? What was a big move in the 1950s is a meaningless move today. What is a large move today may well be eclipsed in the future. In the year 2000, stock prices are so volatile that some stocks can lose half their value or double their value in just one day. Unfortunately, many of these moves occur overnight due to the release of news, earnings reports, or advisory opinions.

Since news travels so quickly now via the Internet, virtually all investors and traders are aware of the news at the same time (other than a few insiders who know the news before the rest of the world does and who use it—

whether legally or not—to their advantage). But since most of us learn the news at the same time as everyone else does, we are often the victims of large price swings, which seemingly give us little or no advance warning.

As a case in point, consider the behavior of Lucent Technologies in January 2000. While the stock was considered by many to be an excellent and stable long-term investment-grade issue, lower earnings due to the inability of the firm to deliver on orders resulted in a severe decline. On January 5, 2000, Lucent (LU) closed at 72⅜, only to close at 52 the very next day, down more than $20 per share. While one might have expected such a decline in a highly speculative issue, the drop in LU was certainly a surprise. (See Figure 3-1.) Day traders who were short the stock fared well indeed. Investors who were long the stock suffered severe losses and had no choice but to take the loss, hold LU for the long term, or buy more to average down the cost.

On January 4, BMC Software closed at 77 and opened the next day at 57 and then dropped to a low of 36 over the next month. But that's what investing is all about. It's about buy and hold, and buy more when the time is right, if you believe in the long-term potential of the stock.

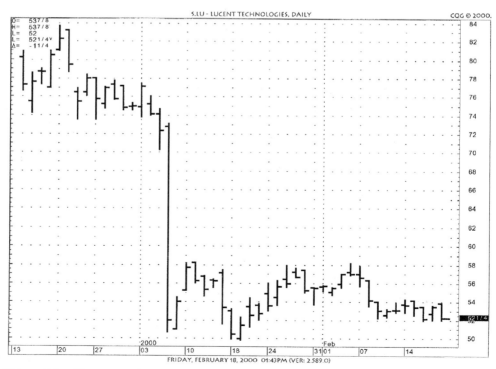

Figure 3-1. The severe drop in Lucent Technologies on 1/6/2000.

In a situation such as the drop in BMC who made the money? Clearly the day trader was unable to make money, since the drop happened on the open. In LU, however, the day trader could have made money since the drop happened within the day. The investor who owned the stock from higher levels lost money (on paper). The only individuals who made money were those who were short the stock. But a lesson can be learned from this simple example.

Although the day trader did not make money, the day trader was spared the loss by not owning the stock. This is one of the major advantages of day trading. By not holding stocks overnight you will not fall victim to declines such as the one in BMC. Clearly, the other side of the coin is that you will not participate in the potential profits of being short or the potential profits of being long when a stock surges on the opening. And there have been many surges to the upside during the last few years.

The day trader must assume that he or she will be left out of such moves, for better or for worse. What the day trader gains in surrendering such possibilities is peace of mind and the ability to turn over his or her investment capital many times by reinvesting it on a daily basis. While there are those who would argue in favor of holding stocks for the long term, there is much to be said in favor of the day-trade approach when it comes to avoiding large overnight moves against your position.

But the other side of the coin is that there are also very large intraday moves in stocks that can be captured by the experienced day trader. In fact, large intraday price moves are more common than large overnight price swings. This is due to the fact that numerous news items affecting the price of a stock can develop during the trading day. Rarely a day goes by without large moves in many stocks.

Yet there are also large intraday moves in many stocks on the New York Stock Exchange (NYSE). Both of these areas will be the focus of our day-trade studies and methods. But do not take it for granted that the only way to make money day trading is by picking stocks that are likely to make large intraday moves. There are other ways that offer just as much profit potential.

Large Moves in High-Priced Stocks

There are more high-priced stocks in the year 2000 than ever before. The mathematics of a high-priced stock are simple. If a $300 stock moves 10 percent in one day, the move is $30, which represents a $3000 move on 100 shares of stock. A $3000 profit on a day trade is a tidy little sum for one day's work. Multiply this by 1000 shares and you have a hefty profit. But 1000 shares of a $300 stock is $300,000.

Few day traders have this kind of money in their accounts. Yet it's still possible to profit handsomely from a $15 price move intraday on 100 or 200 shares. Many stocks in the $100-per-share range or higher can make $15 intraday price swings. And these stocks are the favorites of many day traders. However, as noted, this is not the only way you can make money day trading. There are several other general approaches to the mathematics of day trading.

Small Moves in Low-Priced Stocks

It doesn't take the mind of an Einstein to figure out that large money can be made in small moves if you own a large block of shares. If you trade 1000 shares of a $30 stock for a $3 move, you've made $3000 on an investment of $30,000. As you can see, this is the same amount of money you'd have made on a $30 move owning 100 shares of a $300 stock. The mathematics are simple. But there's even more to the facts and figures.

Could you trade 3000 shares of a $9 stock for ½ point? Yes, you most surely could. In this case, your profit before commissions would be ½ point, or $50 per share × 3000 shares, or $1500. This is the essence of trading large blocks for small moves. Which is best? I think it's all a matter of personal preference and experience. You need to do what you can relate to and what you can understand. There is no hard-and-fast rule. Study some of the methods I've presented and then decide what fits your style, pocketbook, and temperament as a day trader.

Examining the Profit Potential

The two basic approaches to day trading each seek to arrive at the same goal, yet their methods of arriving at that goal are distinctly different. Not only do they require their unique methods of implementation, but, by their very nature, they also necessitate distinct psychological and philosophical orientations.

These two approaches are as different as the retail merchant who seeks to sell a small number of products that are very high-priced and the mass marketer whose goal it is to sell a large number of products at a very small profit per item. In the long run the goal is to make a profit, but in the short run the methods of marketing are extremely different.

The decision to day trade stocks, according to one or both of these methods, is, therefore, not to be taken lightly. While the profit potential from each approach may be similar in the long run, the two procedures are sufficiently different as to warrant serious consideration by the experienced trader as well as the newcomer. With respect to the decision you make, I offer some well-founded advice as follows:

- *New traders:* Those who have never invested in stocks before are strongly advised to begin their day trading in the most conservative fashion. And that would be to trade a small number of shares for larger moves. The prospect of trading a large block of shares (i.e., more than 500 shares) not only may arouse an understandable degree of trepidation, but also may affect the new trader psychologically and behaviorally.

  After a given amount of experience has been attained and a comfort level has been reached, the new trader can go forward into other areas. At first, however, prudence and caution are best.

- *New day traders:*   I make the distinction here between new traders (as in the previous section) and new day traders. New day traders have had experience in the markets before. They have bought and sold stocks, they are aware of the mechanical procedures of order entry, they have an understanding of terminology, and they have a sense of how the markets move.

  In short, they have experience. Their experience will be highly valuable when it comes to day trading. The individuals in this category may even have day traded stocks now and then. And this helps as well. Traders who fall into this category can choose either of the trading alternatives or they may attempt both.

- *Experienced day traders:*   This group may participate in both approaches. Eventually each individual will decide, on the basis of many variables, which approach is best. Of course, the end result may be that both methods are employed. Both approaches will be discussed in detail later.

Evaluating the Risks

Although it seems fairly obvious, risk and reward must always be evaluated at one and the same time. For some traders the risk of losing thousands of dollars in one day, while certainly unpalatable, is acceptable within their financial ability and within the context of potentially larger daily profits. On the other hand, even a $200 loss may be unacceptable to a novice trader, particularly if he or she has come into the markets with unrealistic expectations. We have been led to believe that the larger the potential profit there is for a given trade, the larger will be the potential risk.

I disagree. I believe that the risk in day trading often exceeds the potential reward. This is true because traders tend to operate at the disadvantage of price executions and commission costs. On the other hand, there are some situations (though few and far between) in which the potential profit exceeds the risk of loss. Clearly, the trader who can identify these opportunities and implement them will be successful. Hopefully, the systems, techniques, methods, and indicators in this book will help you find these opportunities.

Those who are new to trading are forewarned that there are no risk-free day trades. Whatever you may have read elsewhere, whatever you may have been told by a friend, relative, acquaintance, or persuasive advertisement, is a lie if it has not covered the essential aspects of risk. There has been a tendency in recent years for promoters to tout the benefits of day trading stocks while minimizing the potential risks. This game is not as easy as many would have us believe. There is risk. The risk can be considerable. And the risk is worse if you have never played the game before.

The Reality of Risks and Rewards

The reality of the day-trading game is that there is a learning curve. Day trading is a business. It takes time to learn it. The education costs you money. And the cost of an education is more than the mere cost of books, courses, or seminars. There is the cost of your investment, the cost of your time and effort, the cost of funding your account, and the psychological cost of trading. These are all important considerations.

Above and beyond these costs you must also consider the value of your time. In other words, your time has value. Could you be making more money doing something else? Are the results of your trading worth the time and effort? Of course, it will take time to reach a level where you can make decisions about these questions. If, however, after a length of time you are not able to generate the kind of money you want, then the approach you are using is ineffective, your discipline and/or procedures are not effective, or you are suffering from limitations in both areas.

How Long Will It Take?

Many newcomers to day trading ask how long it will take to be successful. There is no definitive response to this question other than to state that it takes as long as it takes. There are so many different variables that to state a definitive response would be absurd. In addition, so much depends on the individual that it is impossible to give a specific response.

Generally, however, I would state that if after giving the day-trading venture a year of consistent effort you have not shown an improvement or a positive learning curve, then there is something wrong. Take time to evaluate your approach as well as your implementation so you may determine what's inhibiting your success.

What Causes Large Intraday Price Swings in Stocks?

Large intraday price swings in stocks can be the result of many different factors. Among these are news reports, brokerage house or newsletter writer recommendations, the overall trend of stock prices, specific factors such as earnings, lawsuits, investigations, mergers, acquisitions, and/or news affecting other stocks in the same industry grouping. The factors are so numerous that the average trader may be better off ignoring them than paying too much attention.

Of course, as with most things in life, there are at least two schools of thought. The first view is that a day trader should have access to as much news as possible. Supposedly, knowledge of the news will help the trader profit. This conclusion is not substantiated by the facts, since news is often old news by the time most people know it. The amount of "insider" information in the stock market is vast. Those who are well connected or who have a pipeline to knowing the news before it becomes public can make money. However, this approach often skirts the fringe of legality. I urge you to avoid such situations. Trading on the basis of inside information is often illegal or at least questionable.

On the other hand, if you have access to news as soon as it becomes available *and* if you know how the news will impact a given stock *and* if you are fast enough to take action on the news *and* if you are fast enough to exit your trade when the news has had its effect, then you will likely make money. This book is not about this approach. In fact, I doubt you will be able to find any book that can teach you how to trade this way.

Consequently, I suggest that you isolate yourself from the news, taking refuge in your procedures, methods, systems, and market indicators. Once you have worked with them long enough, you will have the confidence necessary to implement them without regard to the news.

As you may know, the experienced market technician will claim that his or her method of market analysis is sufficiently sensitive to identify stocks that are about to make large moves by simply detecting insider activity through price behavior. While this is indeed the case at times, the fact is that technical analysis of stocks (or other markets) is not infallible. It has its shortcomings (veteran traders are likely smiling broadly at this or they're simply thinking, "*We hold these truths to be self evident*").

The Good News and the Bad News About Trend-Following Systems and Methods

There are literally hundreds, if not thousands, of systems, methods, techniques, and market indicators. Some are more valuable than others. Some are extremely helpful, and a host of others (in fact, the vast majority) are worthless. Many methods continue to be used and touted by traders simply as a function of their mythological status. By this I mean that some indicators are held to be valuable simply because "it has always been that way" or because "Edwards and Magee* say so."

The fact is that, in spite of the scholarly works presented by chart analysts and market technicians in the past, many previously untested ideas fail to provide meaningful information or profitable results when examined under the microscope of historical testing. This is because many of these ideas are not part of a systematic trading approach or methodology. When combined with a solid risk management framework and a specific set of objective rules, timing indicators and chart patterns achieve a new and worthwhile life. While many of the methods presented in this book have been rigorously back-tested, others have been given only cursory examination and still need additional testing and analysis.

Yet, when combined with sensible risk management practices, their validity becomes clear even without extensive back-testing. In order to use my ideas successfully, the day trader will want to adapt those he or she finds appealing, profitable, sensible, and palatable into an overall approach. This is the creative side of day trading. The ability to integrate indicators and methods which have face validity with other indicators and a risk management method into a profitable trading approach is what day traders seek to achieve as a reward for their efforts.

In short, that's what the game is all about! Fortunately, there are many different alternatives or paths you can follow. The multiplicity of choices is beneficial inasmuch as it provides the day trader the flexibility of

*Roberts D. Edwards and John Magee, *Technical Analysis of Stock Trends*, 6th edition, (Boston, MA: John Magee, Inc., distributed by New York Institute of Finance, 1992).

developing a style or method that will suit his or her individual needs and abilities.

A trading approach that has long been held in high esteem is that of trend following. As the name implies, the trader follows an existing path or trend. By trading with the given trend, the path of least resistance is being followed. The trader who follows an existing trend is moving with the flow of traffic and not against it. This, of course, makes it easier to reach your destination. As a concept, trend trading has considerable face validity.

On the surface, trend trading appears a reasonable and logical methodology, and there seems to be no impediment to its promise of profit. After all, if a day trader knows that the current trend is up and if the day trader buys stocks in the uptrend, then it seems only logical that the odds of being able to sell the stock at a higher price at some point during the day are fairly high. And yes, this all sounds very good in theory. However, in practice there are problems with implementation, the most significant of which are *when during the day to buy, when during the day to sell, at what price to buy, and at what price to sell.*

How is the day trader to know that a given price is low enough for buying or that a given price is high enough for selling? Are there specific, reliable, and fairly predictable patterns he or she can observe that may answer these questions? I say, *yes!* And I will teach you some of these in the chapters that follow. Yet it should not be assumed that trading such patterns consistent with the existing trend is the proverbial piece of cake. As you will see, there is much more to trend trading than meets the eye. The good news about trend following is that it can work. The bad news about trend following is that it can fail. One of my goals in the chapters that follow is to help you distinguish, in advance, one outcome from the other.

Trend Following and Forecasting: Similarities and Differences

Still another approach is that of forecasting prices and trends. The trader who attempts to forecast a price is much like the television weather reporter. Numerous apparent facts are taken into consideration, maps are consulted (in the case of traders, the maps are price charts), movements and patterns are analyzed, a forecast is made, and a position is taken consistent with the forecast.

If conditions develop as anticipated, the forecast will be correct and money will be made. Yet forecasts are fragile things, often subject to dramatic change by the appearance of new variables not considered in the original analysis. In such cases an update may be necessary. With the introduction of new information, the strategy may change.

The similarity between models that attempt to day trade stocks using forecasting methods and trend-following methods is that they both seek to make money. The difference is that trend following assumes a continuation of the existing trend, whereas forecasting attempts to determine when, and if, the existing trend will change. And this is a most lofty goal, one that cannot often be attained in market analysis.

While forecasting price changes will become a more successful venture in the future, there are still significant problems with this approach today. The introduction of high-powered, sophisticated artificial intelligence software and massive computer memory will advance market forecasting to heights heretofore unknown. But this goal is still more than a few years away. For the time being, a trend-following approach is the better of the two. Rest assured, however, that trend following is not the only way in which traders can make money.

Breakouts

Still another valid approach to day trading (and to position trading as well) is to buy or sell breakouts. The strategy here is to buy into a stock that has been moving within a relatively well-defined range as it moves out of that range to the upside. In the case of a stock that falls below a defined range, the strategy is to go short.

In effect, the various breakout methods attempt to buy a stock at a relatively high price in the hope that it can be sold later at a higher price. In other words, you buy high and sell higher. On the short side, you attempt to sell low and buy back lower. As noted, there are a number of technical methods which can be helpful in the day time frame for isolating stocks that are candidates for this approach and for timing your entry.

The Assets and Liabilities of a Trend-Following Approach to Day Trading in Stocks

There are some obvious benefits to the use of a trend-following approach in day trading. The first and most valuable advantage is that you are moving with the path of least resistance. In other words, the odds favor a continuation of the current trend. If you trade with the existing trend, then the odds will be in favor of your making a profit. This point has been discussed earlier in more detail. The essence of day trading with the trend is that it is relatively easy to do and is often highly accurate. Nevertheless, it is not possible to consistently win using this general approach unless you have developed or learned a precise methodology that will help you be consistent in identifying such opportunities.

The liability of a trend-following approach is that sooner or later the trend comes to an end. Unless you have a method of determining when the trend is about to reverse, you will be caught in a trend reversal, which will result in your losing money. Determining when a trend is apt to change or when it has in fact changed is one of the critical and ongoing issues in trading. I will provide you with several tools that I believe can be effective in helping you discern such changes in trends, as well as determining the current trend of a stock.

Finally, the use of a stop loss is the single best tool that a day trader has when it comes to minimizing the losses that occur when a trend changes. Unfortunately, too many traders fail to use stops and tend to remain in day trades in spite of the fact that the trend has turned against them. This is, of course, at cross-purposes with the intent of the trading system and it certainly negates all the positive aspects of risk management. Yet it is a fact of market life that cannot be denied.

The Assets and Liabilities of a Prediction-Based Approach to Day Trading in Stocks

As discussed earlier, the predictive method of day trading stocks has severe limitations. There are few predictive methods that have demonstrable value. While there are those who claim that their methods have predictive validity, it is unfortunate that many of these approaches are more artful than objective and cannot, therefore, be subjected to a critical test of their efficacy.

Methods such as those of W. D. Gann, R. N. Elliott, Leonardo Fibonacci, and others are, at best, subject to the kind of interpretation that tends to confound the day-trading issue for many traders. While I do not impugn their potential effectiveness in day trading, I can say that I have not seen anyone use them profitably. These methods do have some valid points to offer; yet they are too subjective for my taste.

How to Determine What's Best for You

As you can see from the foregoing presentations, there are numerous approaches from which to choose your orientation to day trading in stocks.

Certainly you are not restricted to selecting only one method. I find, however, that the more dedicated a trader can be to one method, the more apt he or she will be to learn it well and to use it profitably.

In order to decide what's right for you, the best approach would be to wait until you have learned more about what's available. Determine how much risk is involved in each of the various methods and systems. Determine how much time is necessary in order to implement the various strategies. And finally, determine how much capital is required. By the time you have finished reading this book you should be in a position to make a good number of these decisions. At the very minimum, you should have some direction and a sense of where you want to go with your stock day trading.

Fundamental Versus Technical Analysis

A basic controversy in stock and commodity trading has, for many years, been the conflicting views held by technicians and fundamentalists. Each camp or faction claims to have the correct or best approach to market analysis, forecasting, and trading. Let's take an objective look at the assets and liabilities of each method. In so doing, you will be able to make an educated determination as to which approach most appeals to you.

Let's look at what I call the good, the bad, and the ugly of fundamentals, technicals, and the peculiar offspring of the hybrid approach that one might, for public relations purposes, term *techno-fundamental market analysis*. We will take a critical overview of the two major techniques, and we will then examine their hybrid, technofundamental analysis, in order to see which, if any, might be the most desirable approach.

Please understand that other market experts will take issue with my explanations and conclusions. After all, we all have our differing views of what works best and these views are the result of vastly different experiences. I may be right or I may be wrong, but I will be clear and direct. Although my opinions ultimately may be proven worthless (but I do not think they will), they are designed to stimulate thought, and in so doing, to promote positive change. My opinions are based on considerable experience and should not be dismissed lightly.

Fundamental Analysis

What is a *fundamental?* Indeed, virtually everything is fundamental. Do we mean fundamental as opposed to trivial or fundamental in the sense of basic, or fundamental in the sense of a building block?

A working definition of the term as applied to market analysis might be as follows:

> **A fundamentalist uses historical market-related information to analyze the supply-and-demand aspects of a market in order to determine if the current price of a stock is either too high, too low, or just right in terms of the analysis. To arrive at this conclusion the fundamental analyst studies earnings, profits, sales, inventories, general business conditions, debt, marketing procedures, management, earnings projections, and a host of other factors relevant to the operations of the business in which the given company is engaged.**

The Fundamentalist Must Be Thorough.   The fundamentalist must be aware of as many facts and factors as possible that may affect the business of a given company. While all conditions for a given stock may look favorable, there may, for example, be legal problems, tax problems or other looming negatives that must be taken into consideration. The fundamentalist must know as many of these as he or she can possibly ascertain. The fundamental analyst weights interest rates and the impact of competition from substitutes or new products, and will be alert to changes in consumption patterns as well as per capita income affecting demand.

As you can see, the fundamental analyst must be aware of a plethora of facts. The task which confronts the serious fundamental analyst is massive. Yet if properly and thoroughly implemented, the results can be outstanding. Successful money managers use this approach as their preferred method of picking stocks for long-term gains. There is no disputing the value of such an approach when it comes to investing. But can this method be successful in the day time frame? I think not.

The intraday behavior of a stock, while a function of fundamentals, is more a function of trader emotion, trading volume, "unexpected" news, and a variety of other factors that may not be primarily fundamental in the same sense as the information which is used by the fundamental analyst. The mere fact that a stock has fantastic earnings will not prevent the stock from falling sharply during the course of one day. The mere fact that a stock has terrible fundamentals will not prevent a massive one-day-short covering rally. No amount of fundamental analysis can help in such situations.

Time: Enemy of the Fundamentalist. The difficulty with the fundamental approach for most speculators is that *vast amounts of time and money can be spent to obtain the past and present fundamental information, and to work it into reliable formulations.* To update this data each day on the thousands of stocks listed would be the task of a full-time staff. The individual trader who wishes to use the fundamental approach is in direct competition with the largest money managers, traders, and mutual funds in the world. And they have relatively unlimited resources of information and analysis. In such a competition, the professionals will almost always win.

Furthermore, fundamentals change over time. They can change dramatically in a matter of hours or even minutes. A merger, an acquisition, an accident, a tender offer, a key staff resignation, or other factor can change the outlook for a stock and completely negate expert forecasts. A fundamental analyst must maintain a constant vigil over the stocks being watched.

To review, then:

- *Fundamentals* are the economic realities that ultimately affect the price of a stock.
- *Fundamentalists* are those who formulate a trading plan or trading approach on the basis of fundamentals.

The Roots of Fundamental Analysis. Fundamental analysis has its roots in economics. Since there are many economic theories, there are many different approaches to fundamental analysis. The common element of all approaches to fundamental analysis is that they study the purported causes of price increases and price decreases in the hope that they will be able to ascertain changes prior to their occurrences. Their success rests upon the availability of accurate assessments of the variables they analyze, as well as the availability of variables that may not be known to other fundamental analysts.

The surplus of statistics available to the fundamentalist at any given point in time can be overwhelming. The fundamentalist must be selective and be prepared to evaluate a massive amount of data. There is no one typical fundamentalist. Rather, there are many different types of fundamentalists, who evaluate different types of data at different times. There are those who, by virtue of their skill and their expertise, can provide accurate forecasts, and there are those who, working with the same tools, make worthless forecasts.

Limitations of Fundamental Analysis. The popularity of computer technology has, unfortunately, overshadowed the excellent work being done by many individual researchers in the area of fundamental analysis. The tendency of modern society to look for quick and easy solutions to problems has been partially responsible for the shift away from public implementation of fundamental analysis. On the other hand, the difficulty and complexity of fundamental analysis have, in part, stimulated the contemporary trend toward simpler solutions.

The average investor will have very limited success in understanding, analyzing, and implementing massive amounts of fundamental data. Even if all relevant statistics were available, the average trader would have difficulty interpreting their meaning as it relates to the important issue of trading stocks, which is timing.

Some of the difficulties with fundamental analysis can be summarized as follows:

- *Not all fundamentals can be known* at any given time.

- *The importance of different fundamentals varies at different times.* It is difficult to know which fundamentals are most significant at which time.

- *The average speculator may have difficulty gathering and interpreting the wealth of information* that is available for every stock.

- *Fundamental analysis often fails to answer the important issue that faces most speculators—the question of timing.*

- *Many fundamental statistics are available after the fact.*

- *Fundamentals can be significantly altered by abrupt changes such as politics, mergers, tender offers, legal problems, government policies, interest rates, changes in technology, competition, international events, and some technical factors.* It may take time for these items to be reflected in the fundamental statistics.

- *The amount of effort required in gathering, updating, and interpreting fundamental data may not, in the long run, yield efficient results for the average trader or investor,* whereas the fund manager or well-capitalized trader can do extremely well with such analysis.

- *Most fundamental analysis does not provide alternatives based on price action,* but rather it provides alternatives based on changes in underlying conditions.

- *While fundamentals are important to the investor, they may have very little applicability to day trading.*

- *These changes may be so slow that no visible or perceptible alterations in bullish or bearish stance can be justified,* when, in fact, a major change in trend may have started.

A Definite Place in the World of Stock Trading. Yet in spite of these shortcomings, fundamental analysis still has its place in the world of stock trading. Ultimately, the price of every stock is a function of fundamentals. Fundamentals seek to answer the "why" of market moves. Unfortunately, fundamental analysis has been the whipping boy of market technicians for many years now.

Whether justified or not, this has led to an understatement of its importance. Rest assured that the fundamentals are very important and that their implementation can yield significant results over the long term. I maintain that fundamental analysis has its place for the intermediate- and the long-term trader.

Short-Term Trading, Day Trading, and Fundamentals. For the short-term speculator and/or day trader in stocks, I suggest that fundamentals are not likely to yield the results you seek other than in situations where the immediate effects occur. In other words, if you have advance notice of a fundamental that will be known the next day or the same day, then you can take advantage of it for day trading or for short-term trading. Yet knowing such fundamentals is often impossible unless you're an insider, and then the use of such information for trading may be illegal.

The individual who is willing to establish a major position, stay with the position, give it plenty of leeway, and possibly add to the position on a scale-in basis can do very well using fundamentals. This is the proper place for the fundamentalist.

The long-term trader (i.e., investor) is primarily concerned with timing. Frequently, investors can ride through virtually any market storm since they often employ a buy-and-hold strategy. The speculator, however, cannot use the same approach since his or her capital, time, patience, and tolerance are limited by the constraint of available resources. And the day trader is, of course, bound by the day time frame. Timing must have surgical precision.

Technical Analysis

With the exception of the rank newcomer, virtually everyone is familiar with one or more aspects of technical analysis. Technical analysis is loosely defined as "the study of stock (or commodity) trading data with the goal of forecasting price and/or determining specific market entry and exit."

In simple English, this means that the technical analyst studies such things as price, volume, timing indicators and chart patterns, mathematical or pattern-based trading systems, waves, and trends, as well as their interrelations and combinations. The purpose of studying such relationships is to determine when to buy and sell, to determine price targets or stop losses, and/or to determine when to add to positions.

The goal of most technical analysis is not necessarily prediction; it is, rather, the determination of specific entry and exit levels and/or specific price objectives. Prediction is not a requirement. Yet there are some technical methods whose sole intent is to predict prices and trends. Such methods have their assets as well as their liabilities. In most cases, however, technical analysis methods that provide entry and exit points (i.e., timing) alone are sufficient.

The roots of technical analysis can most likely be found in methods developed hundreds of years ago in Japan. Since technical analysis prides itself on having a quasi-scientific basis, you can understand how the continued exponential growth of scientific methodology has spread into the area of technical analysis (as well as fundamental analysis). As a consequence, there are literally hundreds of technically based systems, methods, techniques, and trading approaches.

Limitations.   Technical analysis has its place in the world of stock trading, yet it has its limitations as well. It is my belief (based on a vast amount of experience) that technical analysis is more suitable for short-term and day trading than for long-term trading or investing. Many of the technical methods discussed in this book, as well as those described in other books on trading, may be applied to long-term trends and investing, as well as to short-term and day trading.

What the Technical Analyst Does.   The technical analyst or market technician has a large arsenal of tools at his or her disposal. Through the years, many tools have been developed to assist the technician in finding points at which to buy or sell. There are several different kinds of technical analysts. For the purposes of this book it is not necessary to discuss the different approaches to technical analysis.

It is only necessary to know that the true technician is not at all concerned with fundamentals or their expected impact on prices. In fact, the pure technician will do his or her best to completely ignore the news and the fundamentals. They have no place in the job of technical analysis. The staunch market technician will argue that changes in the price of a stock can be detected well in advance by a good technical method. Hence, the skilled technician will know that "something is going to happen" in a stock *before* it actually happens.

And I believe that there is a considerable amount of truth in that statement. After all, insiders often know changes in fundamentals well before the investing world becomes aware of these changes. Insiders act on their knowledge (at times legally, at times illegally, and at times on the fringe of legality). Their buying or selling affects the price of the stock and concomitantly its technical behavior.

Technical analysis (using the correct methods) can supposedly reveal coming changes in advance or close to the inception of price moves that occur as a result of such changes in fundamentals. But, as you will see from the list in the next section, technical analysis is not without its weak points or detractors.

Criticisms of Technical Analysis.   There are a number of criticisms that can be directed against technical analysis. Most are reasonable objections that must be addressed and considered when you do your technical market work. These criticisms and potential weak points are as follows:

- *Pure technical analysis ignores all extraneous inputs* such as news, fundamentals, and weather. This is seen as a detriment by some, since these factors can and do significantly affect prices. The response to this purported weakness of technical analysis has been addressed previously.

- *Technical analysis is a form of tunnel vision,* since it accepts input from no other method or technique when employed in its ideal form. Tunnel vision is not a good thing in trading or investing, since it may cause a trader to overlook some important facts.

- *Technical analysis is so widely used, particularly by computer-generated trading programs,* that many systems act in unison, thereby affecting prices in a fashion that is not representative of the true price structure. Therefore, mechanical analysis is a self-fulfilling prophecy and is likely to be ineffective in the long run.

- *Technical analysis cannot allow for good forecasting or determination* of price objectives, since it does not account for underlying economic conditions.

- *Technical analysis is not a valid scientific approach,* since many methods project price trends based exclusively upon price-related data, which does not reveal the important facts behind the success or failure of a company.

- *All price moves are random (called the "random walk theory") and cannot be predicted.*

The Techno-Fundamental Trader

This is the third category of market analysis. Although I will devote very little time to its discussion, it is, perhaps, the category which characterizes the vast majority of traders. This is because in practice there are relatively few pure fundamentalists and relatively few pure market technicians.

Most technicians will consider fundamentals in their analysis. Although they may claim that fundamentals do not enter into their decisions in any way, shape, or form, I maintain that there is a subliminal or unconscious effect on us whenever we are exposed to fundamentals such as news. Since most of us are unable to be completely free of exposure to the news, we are likely victims of subliminal influences and, as a result, our technically based conclusions may not be as pure as we lead ourselves to believe.

And, since news and fundamentals influence most traders, they are not pure technicians and fall into the techno-fundamental category. Note that there is nothing wrong with this type of analysis as long as you are clear about where your trading signals came from.

The Focus of This Book

Now that I have given at least cursory mention of the different approaches to trading and investing, I will tell you that the focus of this book will be near 100 percent technical. I will not cover fundamentals inasmuch as I do not believe that the day trader in stocks can use fundamental analysis with any reasonable degree of success.

My reasons have already been cited. I would add to this the fact that technical indicators which are objective and which can be operationally defined can also be back-tested as to their efficacy and reliability. This is the single most important reason for the use of technical analysis.

Guarantees

While there are many technical methods that can be back-tested, some are not fully testable, yet they are essentially objective. I will do my best to give you a precise evaluation of how well the different methods, indicators, and systems presented in this book have worked in the past. Note that I cannot guarantee the future. How a trader uses technical tools can make the difference between success and failure, between profits and losses.

All too often, traders implement good tools incorrectly or incompletely. They follow ineffective trading procedures, which denigrate the profitability of otherwise profitable tools. This is one of the reasons that prevent me from guaranteeing that the tools will work. Still another reason is that some tools do lose their effectiveness over time. This is why the astute technical trader will continue to develop and test indicators, systems, and methods.

A Few Words About Process and Procedures

I believe that the main reason for trader's losses is that they use poor procedures. By this I mean simply that they are sloppy, disorganized, and not thorough in applying their systems, methods, or indicators. I believe that one of the key ingredients for success is to follow the right procedures.

While trading is not like brain surgery, it does require the application of procedures and methods in an organized and disciplined fashion. The neurosurgeon who fails to follow time-tested procedures may mistakenly leave an instrument or sponge in a patient. The patient could die. The trader who fails to follow procedures will not lose a patient but will likely lose money and in the process may lose so much money that he or she may become a patient (in the psychiatric unit).

While my major goal in this book is to teach you systems, methods, and indicators that can be applied to day trading stocks, my secondary goal, and one equally important, is to educate you in the proper procedures. Knowing how to implement the methods and systems is just as important as knowing the systems and methods. To use a system or method without the proper procedures would be like flying a plane without lessons. There's a chance you could learn by doing, but the odds of crashing first are too high for my comfort. I will, therefore, emphasize the importance of process throughout this book.

I have examined many of the books that attempt to teach day trading. The vast majority of them teach little or nothing. They throw ideas at you haphazardly, hoping that some of them will make sense. They give vague examples and even when their examples are clear and their methods are well defined they often fail to give you precise methods of implementation in a step-by-step fashion.

While some readers may be able to extract the necessary information from these books, most will fail miserably in attempting to implement the ideas without a clear-cut procedure. Don't get me wrong. I think that there are a few outstanding books out there on day trading in stocks. I have read them and I have learned a great deal from them.

You may believe that highly speculative stocks have the potential to make more money than do slow-moving stocks. And I agree with you entirely. Yet there are other strategies for making money in stocks that are not volatile but which can also make you good money. However, as an investor or as a trader you must decide where and how you want to fit into the game.

You can do that only when and if you know your limitations and capabilities. Not all of us can cope with a stock that drops $24 in one day and rallies $29 the next day. This type of trading is not for everyone! What, then, are your choices as an investor? Here are a few of them:

■ *Slow and steady—dollar cost average.*   This is the good old-fashioned way to make money. You do your homework. You research different stocks. You study their earnings, management, sales figures, products, market share, and a host of other statistics. Then you make a decision about their future. If you like what you see, you take a small position. And then you add regularly to that position. It's called investing!

In short, you try to buy low and one day—many months or years from now—to sell high. You could achieve the same result by being a pure technician and only studying the charts. And, of course, you could achieve all of this in the easiest way by buying mutual funds and letting a professional do it all for you (for a fee).

■ *Fast and not so steady.*   This is the more aggressive way to trade. You don't concern yourself with the fundamentals of the company; you simply look at the current price trend. You use a host of technical indicators or even a trading system. You take a position for the shorter term and try to get out at a higher price. You can try to buy low and sell high, but more often than not you buy high and try to sell higher.

And you can trade the short side as well (although in reality most investors or short-term traders do not sell short). Your time frame is considerably shorter than that of the investor. Your approach is not as steady and most likely not as accurate. But you are interested in the faster buck, so you make the concession of lower accuracy.

■ *The day trader.*   You can day trade. The good news here is that you're in and out fast. You don't ride losses overnight, and you make the most use of your trading capital. The bad news is that the vast majority of would-be day traders haven't the slightest idea of how to play the game profitably. Their losses are grist for the mill of the specialist or the market makers and the broker who takes their commissions with a smile and sometimes with a thank-you.

This book is designed to help you profit as a day trader. The day-trading game has often been misrepresented as an easy game to win. It's not. The day-trading game has often been touted as something that anyone with a few thousand dollars and a little common sense can do. And they *can* do it! But the real issue is whether they can do it profitably.

■ *The IPO game.*   This is yet another way of playing the market. Rather than focus on any of the aforementioned methods, you evaluate new stocks and try to buy them when they first begin trading. Your hope is that they'll soar several hundred percent in a few days (if not on the first day) and you'll get out with some fast money.

The good news here is that this method can work quite well in certain market environments. The bad news is that one cannot always get into an IPO and that in the wrong market climate the IPO game has a low probability of success.

- *The covered option game.*   This is a steady and conservative game to play. You own stock and write options against the stock. Since you're a seller of the options, you collect the premium and pocket it. The only way you can lose is if the stock goes against the option you sold and it's taken away from you or put to you.

    Generally, with stocks that don't move much, this can be a good game to play, but the overall returns are not too high.

- *The stock split game.*   This is a fun game when it works. You buy stocks when a split is announced and you get out after they rally on the stock split news. This has been a great game to play in the current bull market. But, when the bull market is over or when it takes a respite, the split game can be a very costly one.

- *More games.*   And there are even more games which you can play in the market. Some make sense, others are foolish, some are very risky, and some are conservative. If you like the short-term approach, there are a number of ways in which you can succeed. But in the long run the most stable approach is to trade for the intermediate to long term. In other words, the most stable game is to be an investor. The short-term game is acceptable, provided you learn how to play it.

As stated, the day trade game is not for most people, no matter what you've been told, what you've read, or what propaganda you've believed. The numerous books on day trading stress the fact that changes in securities regulations in recent years have leveled the playing field. In other words, these changes have made it more feasible for the small trader to compete with the market maker or specialist.

By being able to have his or her orders filled first and at a fair price, the edge or advantage that the specialist and large trader once had is purportedly gone. Don't you believe it! The market makers, specialists, and large investors still have the clear advantage. While changes in securities regulations have given smaller traders the ability to compete more effectively, note that competition is not synonymous with profits. The only thing that has changed is that the system of order execution is fairer.

The professional trader and company will still have the clear advantage by virtue of their experience. The so-called SOES bandit is more of an apparition than a reality. You will still need to compete with the professional trader for your profits and you will also have to compete with an ever growing number of new day traders. The key to success is not necessarily in the ability to compete fairly; rather, it is in perseverance, methodology, technique, and education.

For those who want to play the day-trading game, a little education will save you a lot of money. It might even make you some money. A solid education in day trading will facilitate success, but it will not guarantee it no matter how level the playing field may be. Be careful what game you decide to play in the market. Your odds of success are a function of not only who you are and what you are as a trader, but what game you choose to play and how you play it.

Summary

There have been many large moves in stock prices since the early 1980s. The magnitude and frequency of such moves increases daily. And with increased volatility, the opportunities for short-term and day trading increase. There are many ways in which the day trader can attempt to take advantage of intraday price swings.

None of these will be effective, however, if the trade fails to follow a plan, a system, or an objective methodology. This chapter discussed some of the issues, considerations, and general approaches to short-term and day trading, with an emphasis on objectivity and clear direction, including process as a key variable in the success or failure of a trading plan.

4

The Technical Approach: Timing Indicators, Systems, and Methods

Any path is only a path . . . look at every path
closely . . . try it. . . . Then ask yourself alone,
one question . . . does this path have a heart? If it
does, the path is good; if it doesn't it is of no use.
CARLOS CASTANEDA

As noted in Chapter 2, there are several different methodologies that a day trader can use in the quest for profits. The more common method of determining buy and sell trades by evaluating the bid, the offer, and the size (i.e., number of shares) in order to capture small price moves on larger position sizes was briefly discussed in Chapter 3. This method essentially puts the individual trader into competition with the specialist or market maker. Suffice it to say that with the growing popularity of day trading far too many day traders are using such an approach, hence there is much competition.

The bids and offers for shares of stock based on this approach has become intense and, as a result, it may be only the fastest and most astute traders who are making money using this method. Hopefully my methods in this book will help you do better with less competition. Moreover, I hope that my input will help steer you in the direction of developing your own systematic approach that will not be too similar to the methods or systems of other traders. The present chapter is designed to introduce you to several general technical methods and indicators. I will expand upon these in later chapters.

Timing Indicators, Systems, and Methods

Many traders are not certain about the difference between a timing indicator, a trading system, a trading method, and a trading technique. The following definitions will help you understand these terms. Please read them carefully since they will be used extensively throughout this book.

Timing Indicators

A timing indicator is also known as a *timing signal.* Traders use timing signals and indicators to let them know when a market should be bought or sold. The accuracy or effectiveness of a timing signal is a function of the underlying validity of the idea upon which the indicator is based.

If, for example, my timing indicator is to buy a stock every time it goes down a certain number of points from the previous daily closing price, then the results of what I do will be a function of how well this strategy works. There are literally thousands of ideas upon which timing indicators and signals are based. Some of these have been discussed earlier (see Chapter 2).

The goal of the trader is to find and use timing indicators that have a high probability of success. All too often, traders use timing indicators that are essentially ineffective. Many timing indicators are about as accurate as a coin toss. In other words, their success is questionable. Most of the timing indicators use yield results that are little better than what might be achieved by guessing.

The average trader is unaware of this since most popular books teach timing indicators without giving you an idea or even an estimate of how well they work. Note that a good example of a timing indicator can be found in Chapter 7, "The Open Versus Close Oscillator."

But timing indicators alone are not nearly as effective as they can be when developed into a trading system. See the following section for details on trading systems.

Trading Systems

A trading system is so named because it is totally systematic. It contains specific rules that are operationally defined, precise, and capable of being implemented by anyone who is familiar with the rules of the system. A trading system contains rules for market entry, market exit, and risk management.

The rules are designed to cover virtually every possibility and, if implemented in the prescribed fashion, should allow the trader to reproduce historical performance as long as the system was not fitted to produce the best results. This issue, called *optimization*, is discussed in Chapter 12.

Some traders feel that trading systems are too rigid, that they do not allow the individual trader to exercise his or her common sense and/or experience in trading. This, of course, begs the question of whether traders have common sense, whether common sense is an asset in the markets, and whether experience is of any value when it comes to trading decisions. All of these issues are matters of opinion and have been hotly debated among professionals for many years.

Trading Methods

A trading method is a combination of timing signals loosely organized and implemented according to a variety of relatively general rules. The trader determines when to buy and sell based on his or her rules, yet these rules are often neither highly specific, nor are they sufficiently thorough. This does not mean that the trader who follows a trading method cannot make money.

However, it does mean that a certain amount of subjectivity will enter into the method. Depending on whether you believe that subjectivity is an asset or a liability in trading, you will find the use of a trading method either desirable or unacceptable. In recent years trading methods have come to be known as *proprietary trading.* In using this approach the trader uses a trading method (as opposed to a trading system, discussed previously).

One method which I find valuable and will expound upon in Chapter 8 is *one-hour breakout* (OHB).

Categories of Timing Indicators

There are three major categories of timing indicators. They are as follows.

Leading Indicators. These are indicators that tend to give you buy or sell signals before a market makes its turn. In a sense they forecast a top or a bottom; however, they do not forecast specific price levels or the duration of a move. In theory there are many supposedly leading indicators; however, in practice there are few that truly lead the markets.

A leading indicator, while seemingly valuable at first blush, could pose a problem, since it may get you into a trade too early. In such cases you may have to sit through some movement against you, which in the interim could stop you out.

Time Current Indicators.   These tend to turn higher or lower when the market does. There are many such indicators. They can be very helpful in trading short-term price swings and may, in fact, be ideal for the stock day trader.

While a leading indicator could cost you valuable time in a day trade, a time current indicator could get you in as a market changes direction and out (or in a reverse position) as it changes direction again.

Lagging Indicators.   There are indicators that lag behind the market. They are like the tail of the dog. The market moves and the indicators follow. These indicators are also known as *trend-following indicators* since they follow trends and do not attempt to forecast them. Clearly, their accuracy is limited since they are always late in market entry.

Being late to enter a stock for day-trading purposes is not necessarily a negative quality as long as the existing trend continues. Yet, if you are late in getting in and you enter as the trend is turning in the opposite direction, you will be a victim of the dreaded *whipsaw*.

By this I mean you will be buying at tops and getting out at bottoms—clearly a losing strategy. Hence, lagging indicators must be chosen carefully as a function of their characteristics, or they must be used in conjunction with other indicators that will mitigate this inherent limitation.

The goal in using a lagging indicator is that the trader or investor will be able to profitably grab a significant portion of a trend before the indicator changes direction again. In strong bull or bear markets, leading indicators do excellent work; however, in sideways markets or markets in transition, they tend to lose money and suffer from a low degree of accuracy.

A Confluence of Price and Time

The intersection of time and price is the point at which a stock price changes direction. While most traders throughout the world focus on price, I believe that the price of a market—whether it be a stock, a commodity, an option, a home, or a mortgage—is not nearly as important as the *timing* of your transaction. In other words, I believe that the day trader need not be as concerned about the price of a stock as much as the timing of market entry and exit. Timing is the all-important variable.

While many day traders are good at discerning the trend of a market, their timing is often poor. While many day traders know either intuitively or through experience that a stock will move in a given direction, they are unable to capture any profit from their knowledge since their methods of market entry and exit are often ineffective. They get in too late or too soon or they get out too late or too soon. This is due to either a lack of skill or a lack of methodology or both.

The issue is not really how much you pay for the stock but, rather, whether you got in at the right time. Since you will be out by the end of the day, your goal is not the same as that of the investor. While both the investor and the day trader want to get out of a long position at a higher price than where they got in (or vice versa for short positions), the investor has the luxury of time, while the day trader has a defined time limit. The day trader, therefore, is more concerned about time as opposed to price.

This is not to say that the day trader doesn't care about the price he or she pays for a stock. Price is important; however, good timing can overcome the importance of price. This will become evident to you as we go on, if it is not immediately obvious to you from this discussion. The focus of a day trader must be to move with the existing trend rather than against it. After all, prices that are cheap tend to get cheaper (up to a point), while prices that are expensive tend to become more expensive (up to a point). Trends tend to continue in their current direction. Naturally, every trader has his or her own preference.

Opinions as to what is important vary markedly. Those who focus on time and timing alone tend to ridicule those whose market work is based only upon price. And those who focus only on price find fault with those who consider only timing. In reality, an investment and/or trading approach that combines both elements is likely to be the most productive and profitable in the long run. The coming together, or confluence, of time and price is very important. The day trader who can understand and use both of these effectively is likely to be consistently profitable.

The concept of time and price confluence, when used as a trading system, is a significant and effective approach for making money. Its origin dates back many years. While the concept is valid, putting it into practice is a different issue entirely. Numerous systems and methods have been developed for the sole purpose of putting this concept into practice.

When traders buy at *support* as prices decline in an existing uptrend they are attempting to harness the power of this approach. When traders sell short at *resistance* in an existing downtrend they are employing this concept. In other words, they attempt to combine price with time by selling at a given price when the market rallies or buying at support when a market declines. The day trader who can discern the trend and the price at which to take a position operates with a powerful base of knowledge.

But in order to know when to buy and sell, the traders will need to define succinctly the following market variables:

- *Trend.*   What is the current trend? Is the trend up, down, or sideways? How strong is the trend? Is there a way to quantify the trend? What is the quality of the trend? Is the market moving sharply higher with considerable rapidity and magnitude or is the trend slow and steady?
- *Support.*   If the trend is up, is there a way to determine where a stock should stop its decline when it goes down (temporarily) during a pervasive uptrend? Can a specific price be determined and, if so, how?
- *Resistance.*   If the trend is down, is there a way to determine where a stock should stop its rally when it goes up (temporarily) during a pervasive downtrend? Can a specific price be determined and, if so, how?

The fact is that all three can be ascertained with relative ease. For the time being, suffice it to say that specific methods for doing so will be presented. My intent at this juncture is simply to introduce you to the concept. Here, then, are some methods for determining trends and/or entry/exit points. In each case I will explain the method as well as its assets, liabilities, and variations. An example of each technique will be provided in chart form.

There are numerous books on technical analysis that can explain these approaches in considerable detail. The explanations offered herein are necessarily cursory and are provided only as a general background to the systems and methods I will provide in later chapters.

An Examination of Basic Timing Indicators and Their Applicability to the Day Time Frame

Given the plethora of trading systems, timing indicators, and methods available to the day trader, it is reasonable to expect that most readers will be overwhelmed by the number of choices. Often the amount of information in available texts or online is insufficient to help you make a decision.

In the long run you are left to make decisions on your own. And, all too often, these decisions cannot be made without reference to historical performance. As you can imagine, this poses a formidable challenge to the newcomer. But this is no surprise. All too often, information about what works or what doesn't work in the markets is not available to the public in spite of all the books, seminars, and courses that are available.

Hopefully, the explanations that follow will help elucidate for you the indicators and methods that I feel work best and under what circumstances they do so. I have given you an evaluation of their assets and liabilities, all based on my more than 30 years of experience in the stock and commodity markets.

Moving Average (MA) Indicators: Traditional and Advanced

Whether you use one, two, or many MA(s), the concepts and applications are essentially similar. Either the market price must close above or below its MA(s) to signal a buy or a sell, or the MA(s) themselves must change their relationship to one another in order to signal a trade. Richard Donchian popularized this approach in the 1950s, although it was probably being used well before then.

In the typical MA-based system, signals are generated in one of several ways:

- *Price closes above or below its MA.* Closing above the MA is considered a buy signal, whereas closing below the MA is considered a sell signal.
- In the case of multiple MAs, the approach signals buy or sell signals *when the various lengths of MAs cross one another.*
- In the case of MAs of closing, opening, high, or low prices, signals are generated *when crossovers of the MAs occur as defined by the theory or method.*

Assets

Traditional MA indicators tend to do extremely well in major trends. They can make you a lot of money after a major trend has started if you are able to hold on to your position. MAs are lagging indicators since they give signals *after* a market has made its turn. There are numerous variations on the theme of the MA—some are more effective and responsive than others. Most computer trading systems allow you to use different mathematical formulations of the MA (weighted, exponential, smoothed, displaced, centered, etc.).

Figure 4-1 shows an intraday stock chart with various moving averages plotted against it. Note the rather large differences. MAs can also be used to determine trend. In the traditional approach, price above its MA indicates an uptrend, whereas price below MA indicates a downtrend. In the example provided (Figure 4-1), the stock is in an uptrend after having crossed above its MA the previous day. It remains in an uptrend for the duration of the day.

Liabilities

These indicators tend to give many false (i.e., losing) signals. They will often get you into a move well after it has started, and when a change in trend occurs they will often get you out after you have given back a considerable amount of your profit. Such moving averages tend to be inaccurate and often have considerable drawdown as well as numerous consecutive losing trades.

Solutions

Some of the problems with moving averages can be minimized as follows:

■ *Use a weighted, exponential, smoothed, displaced, or adaptive MA.*

Figure 4-1. Ten-minute Ciena Corp. with five different MAs (28-period).

- *Use a different MA length to exit a trade than you use to enter a trade.*
- *Use different MA lengths for buy signals and sell signals.*
- *Use another indicator to confirm or negate an MA.*
- *Use an adaptive MA.* A more recent addition to the MA arsenal, the AMA tends to be more responsive to price changes by using several variables. To accomplish this, the AMA uses an efficiency ratio (ER) and smoothing constant.

Variations on the Theme of Moving Averages

There are many variations on the theme of moving averages. These include MA-based oscillators such as the moving average convergence/divergence (MACD), the MA channel (MAC), and various high/low MA combinations.

Assets

These variations on the MA tend to be more accurate and more sensitive than simple MA combinations of the closing price. The MACD was specifically designed for S&P trading by Gerald Appel, while the MAC is my creation. Figure 4-2 shows an intraday chart (also Ciena as in Figure 4-1) with the MACD. Buy and sell signals on the MACD are generated when the two MACD lines cross one another. Chapter 11 discusses the use of MACD for intraday stock trading.

The MAC can also be used to determine concise support and resistance levels. It will be discussed in considerable detail as a trading method in Chapter 10.

Liabilities

There is a tendency, as with many MA-based systems, to give back too much profit once a change in trend has developed. This is true of all lagging indicators.

Solutions

Here are some suggestions as to how one might overcome the limitations of MA-based indicators:

- *Use a shorter combination of MA lengths for exit.* Hence, exit will be triggered before the MAs indicate a reversal in trend.

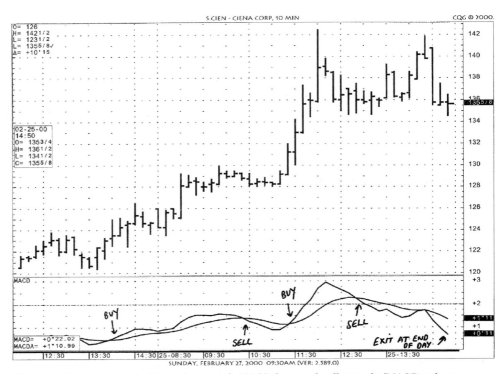

Figure 4-2. Ten-minute Ciena Corp. with MACD buy and sell signals (MACD values = .218, .108, and .199).

- *Use another indicator to confirm the MA signals.*
- *Use another indicator that is not MA based for exiting positions.*
- *Develop a trailing stop-loss plan that will enhance exit* while not significantly diminishing system accuracy.

Stochastic Indicator (SI) and Relative Strength Index (RSI)

Dr. George Lane popularized the stochastic indicator (SI) and its use. The relative strength index (RSI) is essentially similar to the SI. The difference is that the SI has two values, while the RSI has only one. Computing a moving average of the first SI value derives the second SI value. Both indicators are often used to indicate theoretically overbought or oversold conditions. Both may be used as timing indicators as well as indicators of so-called overbought and oversold conditions.

Figure 4-3 shows the 10-minute Ciena chart (as shown in Figures 4-1 and 4-2) with an intraday stochastic and an intraday RSI. There are various methods and interpretations of the SI and the RSI. Some of them are shown on the chart (Figure 4-3). Note that there are many different methods of using the RSI and the SI for the purpose of finding trends, buy signals, and sell signals.

Those included on Figure 4-3 are not being touted as the best. They are merely included as examples for informational and introductory purposes. As you can see, both indicators can generate numerous signals. The number of signals can be adjusted by changing the length of the indicators.

I will elaborate greatly on the use of stochastic indicators in Chapter 6, "Intraday Application of Stochastics."

Assets

Both the RSI and the SI have considerable sex appeal. By this, I mean they look good on a chart. They tend to identify tops and bottoms quite well.

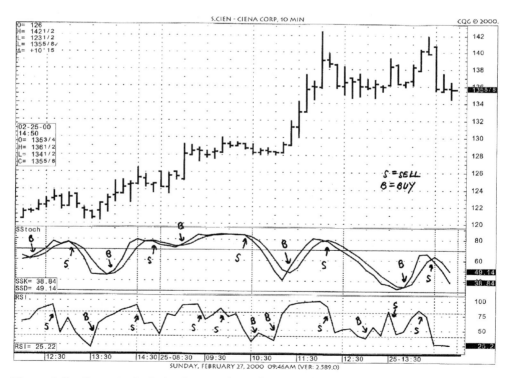

Figure 4-3. Ten-minute Ciena Corp. with stochastic and RSI signals (stochastic 9-period, RSI 3-period).

They are also useful in timing, provided one uses the appropriate crossover areas for timing trades.

Liabilities

The concepts of being overbought and oversold are not useful and are often misleading. Frequently markets that are overbought continue to go considerably higher, while markets that are oversold continue to go considerably lower.

Solutions

- *Don't use the SI and the RSI for determining overbought or oversold conditions.* Use these indicators as timing methods when the readings cross above or below certain values. You might also consider the use of the RSI and the SI with other timing indicators.
- *I have developed the SI "pop" method that may be helpful in trading moves that occur in overbought and oversold territory.* This method is discussed briefly in Chapter 6.
- *Another method of using the RSI and the SI is to exit trades using a shorter SI or RSI length than was used for entry.*

Chart Patterns and Formations

These methods are based on the traditional techniques as proposed by Edwards and Magee, as well as other tools such as those developed by W. D. Gann, George Bayer, and R. N. Elliott. There are many different chart formations and various outcomes possible for each. They require a good deal of study and are at times quite intricate as well as subjective. The commodity trading literature is rich with methods and systems based on these patterns.

Assets

- *These methods are highly visual.* In other words, you can draw lines on a piece of paper, or you can examine patterns visually and see what should be done.
- *The methods don't necessarily require a computer.*
- *They can easily be learned by almost anyone.* Frequently, the prescribed actions

are specific once you have completed the necessary interpretation of the chart patterns.

- *The methods are usually quite logical.* Hence, they have a good deal of face validity.

Liabilities

- *In most cases these methods are highly subjective and difficult to test for accuracy.*
- The Gann and Elliott methods have been known and used by traders for many years; however, *there is considerable disagreement, even among experts, about what patterns exist at any given point in time and, in fact, how these patterns should be traded.*

Solutions

A possible solution would be to use the methods in conjunction with other timing that is more objective and operational.

Parabolic Indicator

This is a method that is based on a mathematical formula derived from the parabolic curve. It provides the trader with two values each day: a *sell number* and a *buy number*. These serve as sell stops and buy stops. Penetration of the buy number means to go long and close out the short, while penetration of the sell number means to close out long and go short.

Figure 4-4 shows the 10-minute Ciena chart with the parabolic indicator. As you can see, there was only one signal and that was to exit the long position entered on the opening and to go short. The long would have been taken on the open since price was above the parabolic sell stop. The day trader would have closed out the short position at the end of the day since the trade was entered as a day trade. In this case the overall result would have been quite profitable.

Assets

- *The parabolic indicator is totally objective.* It can be used as a mechanical trading system with risk management methods.
- *It provides a buy and sell stop daily and is therefore capable of changing orientation from long to short very quickly.*

Liabilities

- *The parabolic indicator can get whipsawed badly in sideways or highly volatile markets.*
- The parabolic indicator can catch some very large moves; however, *it has many of the same limitations that are inherent in the use of traditional moving averages.*

Solutions

- *Use the parabolic indicator with other indicators that are not necessarily based on price—that is, volume and/or open interest.*
- *Use shorter-term time frames for exiting parabolic trades.*
- *Since the parabolic indicator in its pure form is an "always in the market" system, you may be able to adapt it by specifying certain conditions in which it goes into a neutral state (i.e., no position).*

Figure 4-4.   Ten-minute Ciena Corp. with parabolic indicator (step factor .02).

Directional Movement Indicator (DMI) and Average Directional Movement Index (ADX)

These are unique indicators based on reasonable, solid theories about market movement. They are calculated with relative ease and may be used either objectively as part of a trading system or as trend and market strength indicators.

Directional Movement Indicator

The directional movement indicator (DMI) was developed by Welles Wilder. The indicator is used to determine if a stock is trending or not trending. The DMI has three values—the +DI, the –DI, and the ADX—which we will discuss next. Wilder suggests that you *buy when the +DI crosses above the –DI*. He suggests *short sales when the +DI crosses below the –DI*. The ADX is a smoothed version of the directional movement.

Average Directional Movement Index

The average directional movement index (ADX) is a derivative of the directional movement indicator. It measures the *strength* of a market trend, not its direction. The higher the ADX, the more directional the market. The lower the ADX, the less directional the market. The ADX does not measure whether a stock is rising or falling. The overbought/oversold (OB/OS) parameter sets boundaries on the strength or weakness of the *trend*, rather than on the strength or weakness of the *stock itself.**

Figure 4-5 shows one application of the ADX, again on the 10-minute Ciena chart, so you may have a basis by which to compare its signals with those of the other technical indicators.

Assets

These methods are not based on effete concepts or market myths. They are well worth investigating for development into trading systems. The ADX and the DMI are not used by many traders. Their main focus is on the strength of a trend and, as a result, they are somewhat different in their approach. Both timing methods can be very helpful when used in conjunction with other timing indicators.

*For more about the ADX, see Charles LeBeau and David W. Lucas, *Computer Analysis of the Futures Markets,* or Welles Wilder, *New Concepts in Technical Trading Systems* (Greensboro, NC: Trend Research, 1978).

Liabilities

The ADX and the DMI tend to lag somewhat behind market tops and bottoms. As a result, they can give signals that may be somewhat late.

Solutions

- *Use these indicators in conjunction with other indicators that are based on different theoretical understandings of the markets.* The DMI difference is a variation on the DMI. It is the indicator I recommend for DMI analysis.
- *Use a derivative of the DMI or ADX as part of your method.* In other words, compute a moving average of the ADX or the DMI and use the moving average to develop more accurate timing.

Momentum/Rate of Change (ROC)

These indicators are actually one and the same in the final analysis. Although they are derived using different mathematical operations, their output is the

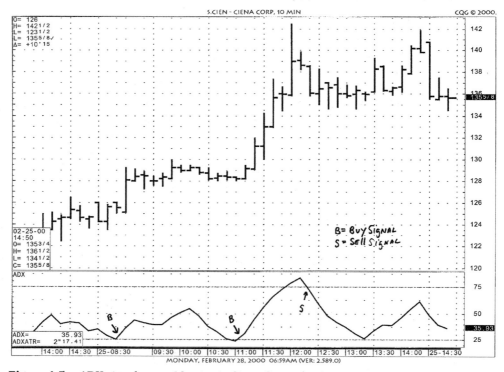

Figure 4-5. ADX signals on a 10-minute Ciena Corp. chart.

same in terms of highs, lows, and trends. I believe that both momentum and ROC have been ignored and underrated as trading indicators and as valid inputs for trading systems.

When momentum crosses above its zero line from a negative reading, a stock is considered to be in a bull trend. When momentum crosses below zero from a positive reading, the stock is considered to be in a bull trend. Momentum can be used in any time frame (daily, intraday, weekly, etc.). Figure 4-6 illustrates one application of momentum, yet there are many more. These will be discussed in Chapter 13.

Assets

■ *These indicators are very adaptable.* Not only can they be used as indicators, but they can also be developed into specific trading systems with risk management.

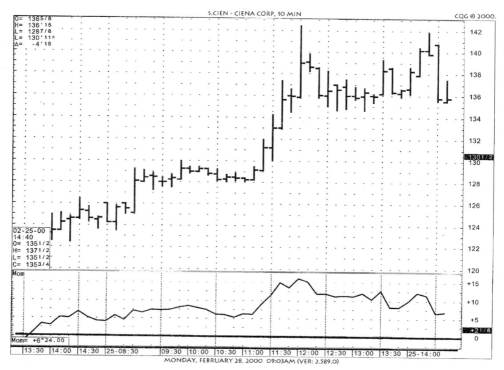

Figure 4-6. Ten-minute Ciena Corp. with 28-period momentum. (When momentum is above zero, the trend is bullish; when momentum is below zero, the trend is bearish.)

- *They can be used with other indicators such as a moving average of the momentum.*

Liabilities

Both indicators lag market turns to a given extent. As a result, they tend to be a little late at tops and bottoms.

Solutions

Momentum and rate of change indicators can be plotted against their own moving averages in order to reduce the time lag of signals.

Accumulation Distribution and Its Derivative

This indicator is one of the more important ones for the day trader in stocks. Although I will explain it more extensively later, I will spend a little more time on it here, given its considerable value. All market movements are a function of the ongoing struggle between those who are bullish and those who are bearish. While the bulls have buying power behind them, the bears have the power of selling pressure.

As long as buyers and sellers remain in balance with no group having clear control, prices remain in limbo, oscillating back and forth but not exhibiting any clear direction. At some point, however, one group gains a clear upper hand and the trend makes a concerted move in that direction.

For many years traders have attempted to find a method that would give insight into the focus of control in a market. Clearly, if we can know which group is in control, we can either buy or sell accordingly with a relatively greater chance that we will be right.

By "control," I mean the balance of power. The question of whether the bulls or the bears are in control of a market is an important one, particularly for the day trader. If we know that the bulls are in control of a market, then we will do well to buy on declines, knowing that the market is likely to recover from its drop. Buying on declines is not a simple matter. There are specific points at which we will want to buy on declines if a market is in the firm control of the bulls. These will be delineated in our discussion of support and resistance.

In a market that is controlled by the bears, rallies will be relatively short-lived, as sellers overpower buyers and the market returns to its declining trend. By *control,* I do not mean to imply that there is an actual group of buyers or sellers who are conspiring to control the direction of a market. Rather, I mean, essentially, "balance of power." In such a market we will want to be sellers at resistance (to be discussed later in this chapter).

In a perfect world we would like to see markets follow our model or theory as closely as possible. While this would simplify our task as traders, it would likely mean an end to free markets since virtually every market trend and trend change would be predictable and there would, therefore, be no markets. Yet we know that this is not the case.

Given the imperfect state of affairs in the stock and futures markets, it would be advantageous to have available to us an indicator, indicators, or systems that would reveal the balance of power in a given market. For the day trader in stocks, such a method would likely prove very profitable if correctly employed.

How could such a method work and what measure of buying or selling power can we use to assist in our task as day traders? Theoretically, as a stock that has been in a bull trend begins to move sideways or makes an abrupt top, a change of control is taking place, as the bears gain the upper hand over the bulls. One interpretation is that selling pressure outweighs buying power. Prices begin to turn lower, yet there is likely advance indication that this is about to happen.

During and prior to a sideways phase, the bears are distributing contracts to the bulls. The bulls eventually reach a point where their cumulative buying can no longer sustain an uptrend and the market drops as the bears continue their selling. Hence, we call this phase *distribution.* Note the example in Figure 4-7, using the accumulation-distribution indicator.

At a market bottom, the reverse holds true. Accumulation takes place as bulls gain the upper hand, overpowering selling by the bears. In theory, buying power outweighs the selling pressure. There is cumulatively more buying than selling. Eventually the balance is overcome, as buying demand outpaces the supply of selling and the market surges higher. The bulls gain firm control and prices move higher.

Theoretically, the bulls are slowly but surely gaining control of the market during the bottoming or accumulation phase. Figure 4-8 illustrates this pattern using the accumulation-distribution indicator.

In spite of our wonderful theories and their face validity, stocks do not always follow their ideal situations. At times a stock will change trend almost immediately and seemingly without notice. Purists will argue that in such cases markets do give advance warnings, but the signs are subtle. I do not disagree. But I note that if the signs cannot be found, then the theory, no matter how seemingly valid, will not help us.

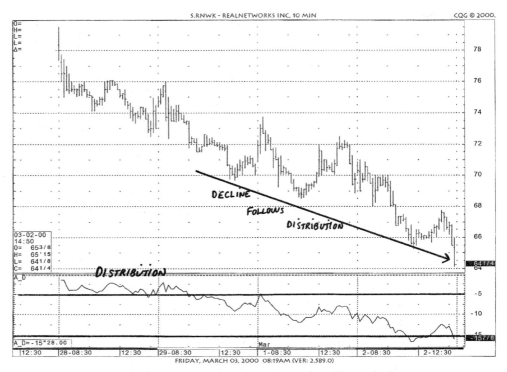

Figure 4-7. Distribution on 10-minute intraday chart of RealNetworks Inc.

The Advance/Decline Indicator

What I have just described for you is the theory of accumulation and distribution. The theory is simple, reasonable, logical, and easy to understand. The difficult part is finding methods, indicators, and/or technical trading systems that will allow traders to take advantage of the hypothetical constructs on both a longer-term and a day-trade basis.

One such indicator is the advance/decline (A/D) oscillator, originally developed by Larry Williams and James J. Waters in 1972. Their article entitled "Measuring Market Momentum" appeared in the October 1972 issue of *Commodities Magazine*. It introduced their A/D oscillator.

The purpose of the oscillator was to detect changes in the balance of power from buyers to sellers, and vice versa. Calculation of the A/D oscillator is a relatively simple matter. A thorough explanation and critical evaluation of the A/D oscillator can be found in *The New Commodity Trading Systems and Methods*.* The A/D oscillator is also available in prepro-

*Perry Kaufman, *The New Commodity Trading Systems and Methods* (New York: John Wiley & Sons, 1987), pp. 102–106.

grammed form on many of the popular software analysis systems, such as CQG (Commodity Quote Graphics) or TradeStation™. The formula for calculating A/D can be obtained either in the original Williams and Waters article or in the Kaufman book (cited here).

Using the A/D Oscillator

There are several potential applications of the A/D oscillator for position and day trading. They range from the artistic and interpretive to the mechanical and objective. While my application may not be as scientific as one would like, my efforts are in the correct direction. One method I have worked with extensively is to buy and sell based on A/D oscillator crosses above and below the zero line.

The construction of the oscillator suggests that when the A/D value is above zero, the market is under accumulation, or the bulls are in control. Conversely, when the A/D value is below zero, the bears are in control of

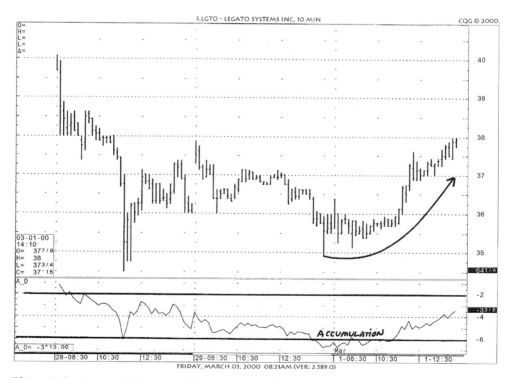

Figure 4-8.   Accumulation on a 10-minute intraday chart of Legato Systems Inc.

the market. Theoretically, when the A/D crosses from plus to minus, a market crosses from bullish to bearish, and vice versa. See Figure 4-9.

Typically, oscillators are used to identify what has been referred to as overbought or oversold conditions. *Overbought* and *oversold* are two terms commonly misunderstood in the markets. *Overbought* refers to a stock or other market (including indexes) that has gone too high. By using the term *oversold*, the implication is that the market has gone too low. On the surface, these terms appear to be worthwhile and reasonable; however, there are no definitive standards for being overbought and oversold.

In other words, a market can seem in an overbought or oversold condition for a long time. Even the term *long time* is subjective. The problem arises when we confuse the terms *overbought* and *oversold* with the terms *top* and *bottom*.

All too often, a stock will move higher and higher while the A/D is in negative ground, and vice versa. Such situations not only confuse the trader into thinking that the theory is incorrect, but they are also costly, since they produce losses.

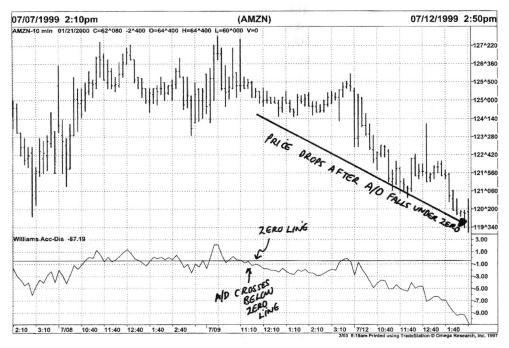

Figure 4-9. Williams's accumulation/distribution (A/D) oscillator on a 10-minute Amazon.com chart.

Yet another limitation of the A/D—and, indeed, of all oscillators—is that they can move back and forth above and below the zero line numerous times before a sustained trend emerges. Traders who buy and sell on such frequent crosses above and below the zero line will suffer numerous repeated losses, not to mention the cost of commissions and slippage. But there's a way to overcome this serious limitation.

The Advance/Decline Derivative (ADD)

The term *derivative* means exactly what it says. It is a value that is derived by a mathematical manipulation of another value. In other words, the first derivative of any number is a new number that is derived from the initial number. If, for example, I have a 24-period moving average as my original value and then I calculate a 20-day moving average of the 24-period moving average, then the 20-day moving average is the first derivative of the 24-period moving average.

If I calculate a moving average of the A/D oscillator, then the moving average I calculate is termed the *first derivative of the A/D* since it is derived from the A/D value. One purpose of calculating a derivative is to smooth the values of the original data. Our purpose is to do this, as well as to use the derivative value and the A/D value for generating signals that will help overcome the limitations of the A/D oscillator when used alone (as cited earlier).

As presented here, the ADD method is objective but not entirely systematic. In order to use it as a system you will need to add a risk management stop loss and/or a trailing stop loss (if you prefer). This will make the method useful as a system. Naturally, you will want to trade the ADD in active and volatile markets only.

The ADD method also has potential for use in day trading. The ADD is a highly versatile indicator, lending itself for use in all time frames. Traders interested in using this approach are encouraged to research it more thoroughly as a trading system with risk management rules before using it extensively for day trading. As an example of how the ADD generates signals, see Figures 4-10 and 4-11. Each shows the ADD with signals on intraday stock charts.

Other Technical Indicators

Perhaps you did not find your favorite indicators included in the preceding section. Know that what you just read is intended to serve as a general introduction. There is much more technical information to follow. If we consider all of the timing indicators that have been developed over the years, as well as the many variations on the theme of these signals, there are literally thousands of possibilities that confront the day trader.

While it's true that the vast majority of these indicators are either useless or specious, there are some that can prove very valuable to the stock day

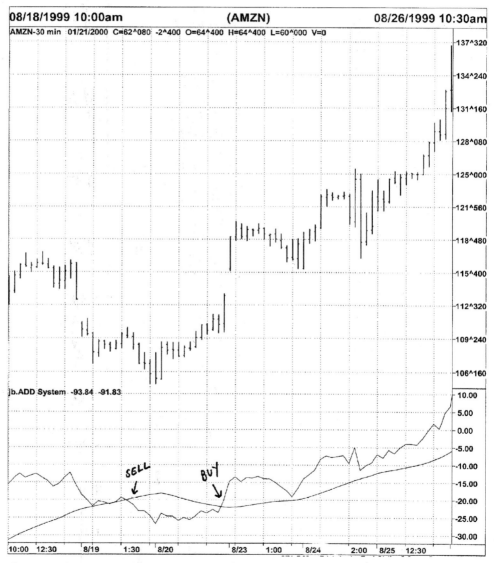

Figure 4-10.   ADD on an intraday chart of Amazon.com, 18 August 1999. (*Chart reprinted with permission of Omega Research Inc.*)

trader. My goal is to alert you to those that I believe to be effective and, moreover, to show how they can be used. In the chapters that follow I will employ some of the indicators cited here as the core of specific trading systems and methods. These will, I hope, assist you in your goal of day trading for profits.

Figure 4-11. ADD on an intraday chart of Amazon.com, 26 October 1999.

Elements of an Effective Stock Trading System

This is the highest and most specific level of trading approaches. As noted in my previous discussion on trading systems, a trading system provides features that make it preferable to all other methods of trading. An effective system will tell you which stock to trade, when to buy, when to sell, how much to risk, and much more. While some traders prefer to use indicators and methods as opposed to systems, I believe that using a system will give you the greatest odds of success.

Here are the essential elements that an effective stock day-trading system must contain (as a point of information, these factors also apply to trading systems that seek to capture longer-term moves as well):

- It contains purely objective rules for market entry and exit.
- It contains risk management rules such as stop loss and trailing stop loss.
- It tells you which stocks to trade and when to trade them.
- It can be back-tested using the indicated rules in order to test its validity.
- Its signals are not subject to interpretations—they are operational, totally objective, specific, and repeatable.
- Historical back-test performance provides key statistics and hypothetical results.
- Different traders should be able to get exactly the same signals using similar inputs.

There are other fine details that characterize a trading system; however, those indicated here are the most important. Clearly, the good news about trading systems is that they can be implemented specifically and without interpretation. The bad news for many stock day traders is that they are unable to follow a trading system due to their lack of discipline. They would much rather wallow in subjective indicators than to have the self-confidence and self-discipline to trade a mechanical system. This book will present several day-trading systems for stocks, yet no matter how good they may look on paper or in back-testing, they will prove totally useless or even unprofitable to the trader who lacks discipline and consistency.

Support and Resistance Concepts

Perhaps the single most valuable tool that a day trader can possess is the ability to determine support and resistance. My working definition of *support* as it applies to trading is as follows:

> **The price level at which a market is expected to halt its declining trend and from which prices are expected to move higher at best or sideways at worst.**

As you can see, this is a purely pragmatic definition. It is tailor-made to the task at hand. But I hasten to add here that support, in and of itself, is not particularly useful unless it is combined with a knowledge of the existing trend. In an *uptrend* the support level or area of a stock is likely to halt a short-term decline within the existing trend. Market technicians have developed numerous ways in which to determine support. The most common of these is to draw support trend lines under the price of a stock. While this can be effective, it is too subjective and often fails to provide sufficient information.

Other methods for determining support are based on percentage retracements, moving averages, previous highs and lows, reversal levels, waves, angles, Fibonacci numbers, market geometry, and a host of other devices, some seemingly logical and others that smack of superstition or magic.

I will avoid most of the common and popular methods in favor of several that I have developed over the past 30 years which I believe to be highly effective. However, I do not expect you to merely take my word as gospel. I suggest you critically evaluate my methods by watching them and seeing for yourself whether they can be helpful to you in your trading.

As an example of support, consider Figure 4-12. This figure shows a 10-minute chart of Emulex with my calculated support line. You will notice how the price of this stock continues to bounce off support during the day. This is the ideal way in which a valid support line should work in an uptrend.

Conversely, resistance is an important consideration in a downtrending market. *Resistance* is defined as follows for our purposes:

> **The price level at which a market is expected to halt its upward trend and from which prices are expected to move lower at best or sideways at worst.**

As in the case of support, there are literally hundreds of ways which traders have developed for determining resistance. The vast majority of them are ineffective. Yet we must remember that the use of resistance (and support) is typically part of a trading method and is not always systematic. Hence, the availability to make money using resistance and support is, to a great extent, a function of the trader's skill level and experience. Figure 4-13 shows an example of how prices act when they hit resistance in a downtrend.

The Value of Day Trading with Support and Resistance

Support and resistance are valuable tools for the day trader. Knowing support and resistance levels, as well as the existing trend, can allow the day trader to accomplish the following goals:

- To buy at or near support in an uptrending market and to take profit either at a predetermined objective or at resistance

- To sell short at or near resistance in a downtrending market and to take profit either at a predetermined objective or at support

- To avoid markets that are either trendless or whose trading range is insufficient to allow reasonable intraday price movement

- To buy a market when it overcomes resistance and, therefore, to go for a larger profit inasmuch as the uptrend is likely to remain strong since resistance has been overcome

- To sell a market when it falls below support and, therefore, to go for a

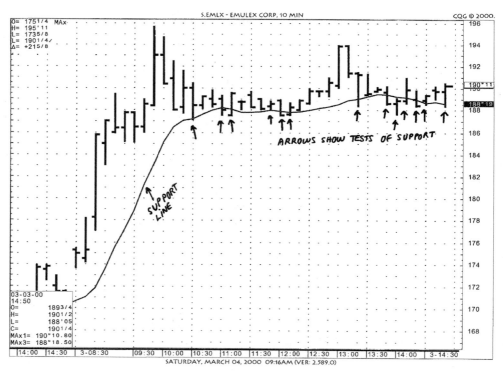

Figure 4-12. Support on 10-minute Emulex Corp. chart.

larger profit since the downtrend is likely to remain strong now that support has been penetrated

In order to achieve these goals, the trader will need to know, as precisely as possible and with as much accuracy as possible, the current trend, the current support level, the current resistance level, and when a change in trend has taken place.

While these seem simple enough, they are lofty goals, not easily attained unless one uses the right methods. A good portion of what follows in this book will address the germane issues I have just cited.

Summary

This chapter examined, in overview, a number of essential concepts in the area of technical analysis and day trading. Key concepts were defined. Numerous timing indicators were introduced. Later chapters will expand on the indicators discussed in this chapter.

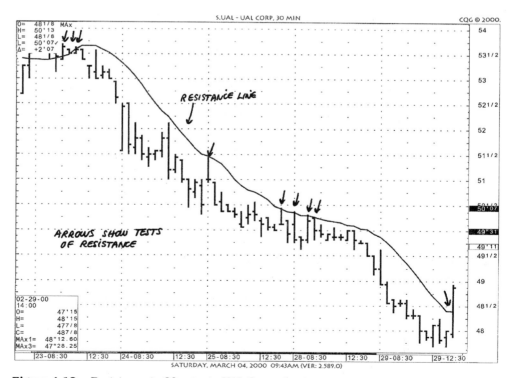

Figure 4-13. Resistance in 30-minute UAL Corp. chart.

5
Gap Methods for Day Trading

Bad news reveals the character of change; good news does not.

MARSHALL MCLUHAN

A price gap occurs when a given stock *opens* at a price that is either above the high of the previous day or below the low of the previous day. While *gaps* do not occur too often (perhaps once monthly on average in higher-priced stocks and even less often in lower-priced stocks), there are so many stocks that can be traded based on gaps. It is valuable for you to learn the gap methods discussed in this chapter.

The beauty of using a gap method for day trading stocks is that you do not need to have live quotes and, furthermore, that the amount of time you need to watch the market is limited. You could actually trade the gap methods in this chapter with only limited attention to the markets. This last statement will become clear to you as you learn the method.

What Does a Gap Look Like?

When viewed on a chart, opening price gaps are relatively simple to spot. As previously defined, a price gap occurs when a market opens either above the previous daily high or below the previous daily low. Figure 5-1 shows a daily chart of Ford Motor Company with the gap openings marked as follows: **U** for gap *up* open, **D** for gap *down* open.

As you can see, gap openings are not too frequent, yet they are significant inasmuch as a gap lower or higher opening reveals an underlying condition of the given market. The significance of the gap will be discussed later. This section merely defines the gap and illustrates it in chart form so you can learn to easily identify opening gaps.

A common point of confusion is that traders often mistake a gap opening from the close of the previous day as a gap opening. This is not correct! For the purpose of your work, a gap opening is measured from either the high of the previous day or the low of the previous day.

Note also that we *do not consider after-hours trading* as part of the trading range. We completely ignore prices from after-hours trading. We take into consideration *only* prices that occur within the trading day as defined by exchange trading hours, which, as of this writing, are from 8:30 a.m. central time to 3 p.m., central time.

Simplicity and the Gap Trade

My years as a trader and market analyst have convinced me that the more input a trader has available in the development of a trading decision, the

Figure 5-1. Gap openings in Ford Motor Company daily chart (**U** = gap up, **D** = gap down).

more likely it is that the decision will be wrong. While this may not sound right, the fact is that it *is* right.

Too much information and too much input can often result in losing decisions. When traders use too much information in making a decision, they cannot help but have their wishes, emotions, expectations, fears, and dreams interfere in the process. Therefore, the more a trader thinks about a trade—the more a trader *analyzes* a trade—the greater the probability that the trade will be a loser.

I do not mean to denigrate the importance of information, yet facts are facts. Unless you're an exceptional trader, you will find, more often than not, that the more you think about a trade, the less you may reap in profits. Day traders don't need complicated systems; they need simple systems that don't require a great deal of judgment or thought. Their systems must be simple enough to generate signals quickly and profitable enough to make day trading worthwhile.

Unfortunately, many day traders are addicted to their quote screens, watching every tick as if their lives were in the balance. I believe that day trading should be a simple proposition, reasonably mechanical, and as objective as possible. Hence, the gap trade and its variation (to be discussed later in this chapter) are ideal for the day trader.

What Causes Gaps?

Gaps can be caused by a variety of factors. The one element common to most gaps is that they occur as a result of news that affects a given market or stock. If, for example, a company releases much lower earnings than expected, and if the market is closed when said earnings are released, the odds are that the stock will open lower and that the lower opening will be below the low of the previous day's low.

Conversely, the release of very positive earnings may result in a gap higher opening. In today's news-rich environment, there are numerous factors that can result in a gap up or down opening. Among these are brokerage house or advisory recommendations to buy or sell a given stock and announcement of a buy order, tender offer, merger, stock split, large order, new technological breakthrough, resignation, or hiring of key corporate personnel. Other factors include lawsuits, government investigations into a given stock, insider buying or selling, earnings announcements, spin-offs, political changes in a given country that may be a larger customer of the given company, dividend announcements, as well as a variety of other items.

The actual cause of a gap trade is psychological. Gaps occur when traders and investors have an emotional response to a given news item or other development with regard to a given stock or group of stocks. If, for example, a statement from the Food and Drug Administration (FDA) suggests that some drug manufacturers may get their new drugs approved more quickly, then all drug stocks in the relevant category may jump sharply higher the next day on the opening, thereby creating a gap.

The gap is, more often than not, an overreaction and, as a consequence, markets can often move opposite from their gap opening. In other words, the given stock opens above or below the previous daily high or low due to panic buying or selling. Then, once some sense of sanity has returned to the stocks, it begins to move the other way, often closing *opposite* from the direction of the opening gap. The process by which this happens is easily understood. The specialist or market maker in the stock that opens gap up or down may often take an opposite position from the way a stock opened. When demand for a stock is very high, the market maker will ration the stock by selling it at higher and higher prices, depending on demand for the stock.

This is a short-term opportunity for the specialist to make a few points on a stock, since the stock will likely move in the opposite direction from its opening gap. When a stock opens below the previous daily low, the market will take advantage of the lower opening by buying shares being sold in distress. Soon sanity returns and the stock moves higher, allowing the market maker to unload these shares at a profit.

A very important point to note at this juncture is that gap higher or lower openings are *not always resolved* by a move in the opposite direction. At times, a stock will open gap up or down and continue to move in the direction of the opening without turning in the opposite direction. The gap will *not be filled.* By this I mean that the stock will *not* change direction and come back down or up. A gap will be left on the chart.

But in such cases, the gap trade technique will keep us from taking a trade (as you will see from the explanation of gap trade rules). In such cases, chartists refer to the unfilled gap as a *breakaway gap.* Such gaps often reveal the longer-term fundamental condition of a market. In other words, a breakaway gap to the upside often indicates a very bullish market, and vice versa for a breakaway gap down.

Figure 5-2 shows a daily price chart of Red Hat Inc., with the upside breakaway gaps marked. As you can clearly see, a series of breakaway gaps to the upside early in the history of this stock was a precursor or leading indicator of strong demand and a major bull move. Figure 5-3 shows an opposite situation. Downside opening gaps that were unfilled predicted a bearish move in Xerox.

As you can see, not only opening price gaps can be used to indicate or signal a possible day trade, but they also reveal other valuable market information, often very early in the inception of a move. Furthermore, once a move in a given direction has started, unfilled gaps in the direction of the move will also tell you that the move is likely to continue in its given direction.

Origin of the Gap Trade

The *gap trade* was originally developed for use in the commodity futures markets by trader Larry Williams, who called it the "oops" signal (for reasons I'll explain later).

The rules of application for a gap trade are simple, but before detailing them I'll illustrate and refine my definitions for you.

1. *Opening gap higher (gap up).*   This occurs when the opening price for the

Figure 5-2.   Upside breakaway gaps and subsequent bull move in Red Hat Inc. (arrows mark breakaway gaps).

day is higher than the high of the previous day. See Figure 5-4 for an ideal representation of the *gap higher* open. Note that when I refer to the "opening," I mean the first "print" price, or the officially defined opening as determined by the given exchange.

2. *Open gap lower (gap down).* This occurs when the opening price for the day is lower than the low of the previous day (see Figure 5-5). Again, by the opening I mean the first print price of the officially defined opening as determined by the given exchange.

   The opening gap up sets the precondition for a *short sale.* The opening gap *down* sets the precondition for a buy. Note that a gap up opening does not immediately signal a buy—it merely sets the first condition for a buy signal. In order for a trading signal to occur, a penetration of the previous daily high or low must occur as the stock moves back down (after a gap up opening) or back up (after a gap down opening).

Note the gap buy and sell signals on a daily chart of Yahoo! Inc. in Figure 5-6.

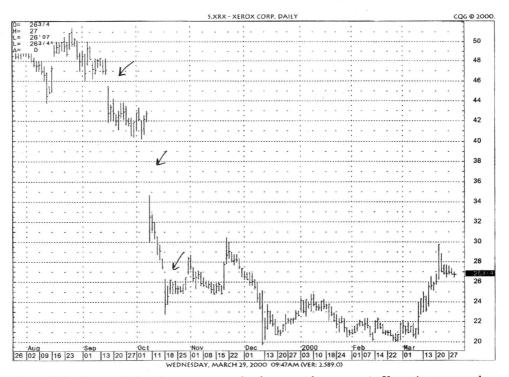

Figure 5-3. Downside breakaway gaps and subsequent bear move in Xerox (arrows mark breakaway gaps).

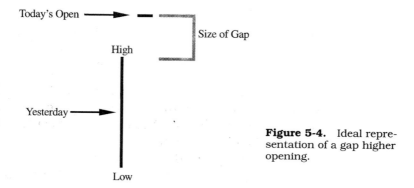

Today's Open

Size of Gap

High

Yesterday

Low

Figure 5-4.   Ideal representation of a gap higher opening.

How a Basic Gap Buy Signal Is Established

A basic gap buy signal occurs when a market opens on a *gap down* and then comes back up to penetrate the previous day's low by a given number of price ticks. By *price tick*, I mean minimum fluctuation. Although stocks can and do trade in fractions lower than ¹⁄₁₆ (referred to as a *teenie*), we will consider ¹⁄₁₆ of a point as a tick, or as the smallest increment in which a stock trades.

When this occurs, you *buy* for a day trade. You exit your trade either at a fixed-dollar-amount stop loss, a stop loss below the low of the day when you are filled, or you exit on the close of trading. A gap trade is a day-trade technique. Trades are not held overnight. Note the ideal gap buy signal in Figure 5-7.

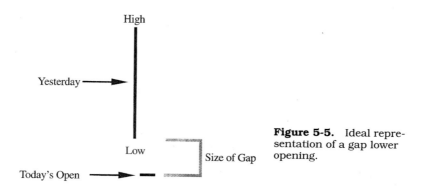

High

Yesterday

Low

Size of Gap

Today's Open

Figure 5-5.   Ideal representation of a gap lower opening.

A Few More Details

As you can see, the rules of application for the gap trade are very clear, and the application of this methodology is simple. Figures 5-7 and 5-8 show ideal gap buy and sell signals, respectively. Figure 5-9 shows actual gap buy and sell signals in e-Bay.

It should be noted that, when trading in gaps, use only the *day session* prices. I repeat: In determining whether a gap has been made or not, do not use the overnight or after-hours market data. Gaps are determined based on day session data only! This is very important.

Results and Expectations

Figure 5-10 shows my back-test of the gap trades in e-Bay from 09/23/1998 to 03/02/2000. As you can see, the gaps, according to the rules of application, were correct nearly 60 percent of the time, generating a fairly good net profit (before commissions) with a reasonable number of trades. The results

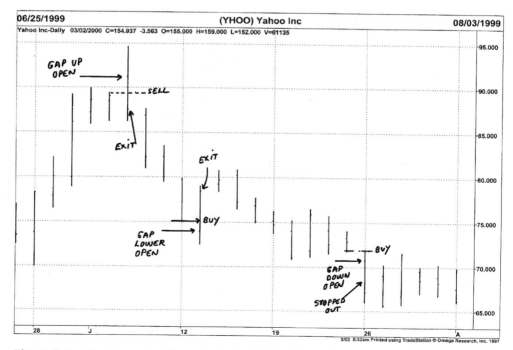

Figure 5-6.   Gap buy and sell signals on daily Yahoo! Inc. chart.

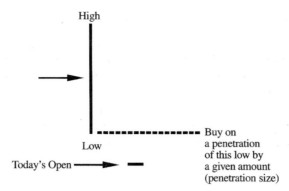

Figure 5-7. Ideal gap buy signal.

here, of course, represent an ideal situation. Actual results may be somewhat better or worse, depending upon where your buy and sell orders are filled.

Other Variables of the Gap Trade

I believe that the gap trade method is a viable method for day trading in active and volatile markets, yet not all gaps are created equal. Some are quantitatively different from others. In other words, there are several other characteristics of opening gaps that are relevant to the effectiveness of a gap. They are as follows.

Gap Size

The size of the opening gap is important. By *gap size* I mean the number of points that a stock has opened above the previous high or below the previ-

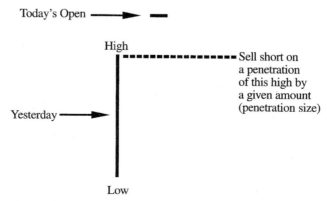

Figure 5-8. Ideal gap sell signal.

ous low. A stock can open only a few ticks above the previous high or below the previous low, or it can open a few dollars above or below the previous high or low. There is a tendency for higher-opening gap sizes to produce a larger average profit per trade than smaller gap sizes.

A more effective approach is to use a different-size opening gap for buy signals than for sell signals. Since markets are not linear, this makes a great deal of sense. By varying the parameters, you will be able to fine-tune the gap trade method for a variety of markets. The mere fact that a gap has occurred does not necessarily mean that the gap will be filled. Frequently, opening gaps are not filled and, as a consequence, a trade is not triggered. Figure 5-11 illustrates a number of filled (**F**) and unfilled (**U**) gaps in Amgen, Inc.

Gap Penetration Size

This variable is also important. It measures how much the market penetrates back into its previous daily range for buy and sell signals. In other words, a smaller penetration size will give you more trades. However, is it possible that a larger penetration size will give fewer trades but with higher accuracy?

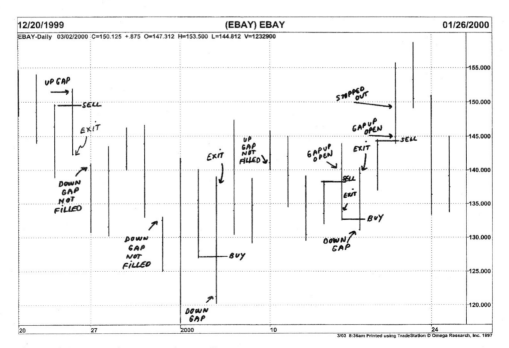

Figure 5-9. Actual gap signals in e-Bay.

```
        jb.Gap System  EBAY-Daily   09/23/1998 - 03/02/2000
                  Performance Summary:  All Trades
```

Total net profit	$21062.80	Open position P/L	$0.00
Gross profit	$33187.40	Gross loss	-$12124.60
Total # of trades	36	Percent profitable	58%
Number winning trades	21	Number losing trades	15
Largest winning trade	$4550.00	Largest losing trade	-$1812.40
Average winning trade	$1580.35	Average losing trade	-$808.31
Ratio avg win/avg loss	1.96	Avg trade(win & loss)	$585.08
Max consec. winners	5	Max consec. losers	4
Avg # bars in winners	0	Avg # bars in losers	0
Max intraday drawdown	-$3025.00		
Profit factor	2.74	Max # contracts held	200
Account size required	$3025.00	Return on account	696%

```
             Performance Summary: Long Trades
```

Total net profit	$13937.00	Open position P/L	$0.00
Gross profit	$21324.60	Gross loss	-$7387.60
Total # of trades	19	Percent profitable	58%
Number winning trades	11	Number losing trades	8
Largest winning trade	$4550.00	Largest losing trade	-$1650.00
Average winning trade	$1938.60	Average losing trade	-$923.45
Ratio avg win/avg loss	2.10	Avg trade(win & loss)	$733.53
Max consec. winners	8	Max consec. losers	3
Avg # bars in winners	0	Avg # bars in losers	0
Max intraday drawdown	-$2800.00		
Profit factor	2.89	Max # contracts held	200
Account size required	$2800.00	Return on account	498%

```
             Performance Summary: Short Trades
```

Total net profit	$7125.80	Open position P/L	$0.00
Gross profit	$11862.80	Gross loss	-$4737.00
Total # of trades	17	Percent profitable	59%
Number winning trades	10	Number losing trades	7
Largest winning trade	$2325.00	Largest losing trade	-$1812.40
Average winning trade	$1186.28	Average losing trade	-$676.71
Ratio avg win/avg loss	1.75	Avg trade(win & loss)	$419.16
Max consec. winners	5	Max consec. losers	2
Avg # bars in winners	0	Avg # bars in losers	0
Max intraday drawdown	-$3374.80		
Profit factor	2.50	Max # contracts held	200
Account size required	$3374.80	Return on account	211%

Figure 5-10.   Gap signals/e-Bay performance summary. (*Reprinted with permission of Omega Research Inc.*)

A stock that opens gap up and then comes down only a few teenies below the last daily high may not be as good a short sale as a stock that opens on a gap up and then penetrates the last daily high by a full point. The larger the penetration size required before you enter a gap trade, the fewer trades you will have but the more accurate they are apt to be.

For examples, Figure 5-12 shows the results of two different studies on Yahoo! Daily (all trades and long trades).

Stop-Loss Size

Stop-loss size is also very important. The typical gap day trade should carry a stop loss large enough to give the market room but small enough to keep your risk reasonable. Typically, a dollar risk stop is recommended. It is important to strike an effective balance between the degree of risk you want to take and the size of the stop loss. Using a stop loss that is too small will be an open invitation to get stopped out repeatedly, whereas using a stop loss that is too large will result in your taking losses that are too big.

Figure 5-11. Filled (**F**) and unfilled (**U**) gaps in Amgen, Inc.

```
jb.Gap System   YHOO-Daily    04/12/1996 - 03/31/2000
```

                    Performance Summary: All Trades

Total net profit	$ 17293.50	Open position P/L	$ 0.00
Gross profit	$ 68574.00	Gross loss	$ -51280.50
Total # of trades	102	Percent profitable	69%
Number winning trades	70	Number losing trades	32
Largest winning trade	$ 6690.00	Largest losing trade	$ -5475.00
Average winning trade	$ 979.63	Average losing trade	$ -1602.52
Ratio avg win/avg loss	0.61	Avg trade(win & loss)	$ 169.54
Max consec. winners	25	Max consec. losers	7
Avg # bars in winners	2	Avg # bars in losers	4
Max intraday drawdown	$ -15325.50		
Profit factor	1.34	Max # contracts held	1
Account size required	$ 15325.50	Return on account	113%

                    Performance Summary: Long Trades

Total net profit	$ 24149.00	Open position P/L	$ 0.00
Gross profit	$ 47168.50	Gross loss	$ -23019.50
Total # of trades	57	Percent profitable	77%
Number winning trades	44	Number losing trades	13
Largest winning trade	$ 6690.00	Largest losing trade	$ -5475.00
Average winning trade	$ 1072.01	Average losing trade	$ -1770.73
Ratio avg win/avg loss	0.61	Avg trade(win & loss)	$ 423.67
Max consec. winners	21	Max consec. losers	6
Avg # bars in winners	2	Avg # bars in losers	4
Max intraday drawdown	$ -6975.50		
Profit factor	2.05	Max # contracts held	1
Account size required	$ 6975.50	Return on account	346%

Figure 5-12.   Results of two different studies on Yahoo! Daily (all trades and long trades).

The Best Gap Trades

You might think that the best gap trades (what I consider the most profitable and most reliable) occur consistent with the extant trend. This is not necessarily true. Some of the best buy gap trades occur in bear markets as short covering panics occur. Some of the best sell gap trades occur in bull markets as traders take profits en masse.

Gap trades have had a noteworthy history. They are reliable and often profitable because they're based on the essential principle that underpins all trading psychology. As long as traders trade markets and as long as traders are human, gap trades will continue to work. And if they stop working, then I'm certain other psychologically based trading patterns will take their place.

Here is a review of the basic gap trade rules:

- To trade gaps, the market must open either above the previous daily high or below the previous daily low by a given number of ticks or points.

- A gap buy signal is generated once the market has opened on a gap lower and then comes back up to penetrate the previous daily low by a given number of ticks.

- A gap sell signal is generated once the market has opened on a gap higher and then comes back down to penetrate the previous daily high by a given number of ticks.

- Gap buy or sell trades are closed out at the end of the day or at a predetermined stop loss.

Pragmatic Considerations in Trading Gaps

Theory is one thing, but reality is another. The reality of gap trading is that it is not appropriate in all markets and it is not appropriate at all times. The fact is that the two most important day-trading criteria must be met if the gap is to be used effectively: volume and volatility. Gap trades based on my rules can work well in volatile stocks, but they are doomed to failure in markets that have small daily trading ranges, where trading volume is thin, and where volatility is minimal (most of the time).

Another practical consideration is the use of stop losses. As you well know, there are three schools of thought on stop losses:

1. The best stop loss to use in a market is a risk management stop. In other words, risk a certain amount of money on each trade, and if the stop is hit, then exit.

2. A stop loss should be determined on the basis of your system and not on the basis of dollar risk.

3. A trailing stop loss should be used once a given profit target has been hit, in order to preserve the profit.

These, then, are the basis stop-loss strategies. Naturally, there are variations on the theme; however, my research has clearly indicated the following best strategies for gap trades as well as for most day trades.

- A dollar risk management stop loss is best as an initial stop.

- Once a given profit level has been achieved, a trailing stop loss is effective.

- The trailing stop loss must be a large one. In other words, you must be willing to risk up to 90 percent of your open profit, or you will be stopped out repeatedly.

- Small stop losses will work against you in gap trades and, in fact, a small stop loss will work against you in virtually all types of trading other than "scalping."

In some cases, holding a gap trade overnight may prove more profitable than exiting at the end of the trading session. But note that the trade would then no longer be considered a day trade. This method will be discussed later in this chapter.

Period of Gap Comparisons— Multiple-Day Gap Signals

While the gap trade has good promise as a day-trading method, there are other possibilities. If you're interested only in day trading stocks as opposed to short-term trading, then don't read the next section. However, if you're willing to hold your trades beyond the end of the day—perhaps for a few days longer—the promise of considerably larger potential profits is what awaits you.

Consider the fact that a gap can be referenced back to the previous day or to any number of days back. Also consider the fact that a gap trade can be held longer than the day time frame. Here are a few worthwhile twists on the gap method that may interest you. As noted, these *require holding beyond* the day time frame and are not, therefore, day trades.

The Multiple-Day Gap Signal (Multigap)

The traditional or basic buy/sell gap signal has already been discussed in this chapter. The gap approach has merit; however, there is a variation on the theme of the gap trade method that may prove even more valuable. While the basic gap method is designed for day trading, there is a way to capitalize on the gap idea for short-term trades. The multigap is also useful for day trading, where the accuracy and average trade increases.

As you know, the basic gap signal occurs when a market opens below the low of its previous day and then penetrates the low on the way back up (buy signal). It can also occur when a market opens above the high of its previous day and then penetrates the high on the way back down. Entry is made on a buy or sell stop, and exit is on the close of trading. In volatile stock markets such as the higher-priced tech, Internet, and biotech stocks, this methodology has merit and back-tests profitably in many stocks.

The Multigap Explained.   The multigap is a simple method. Rather than generate a signal based on an opening gap above or below the previous day's high or low, the signal is generated based on an opening gap above or below the highest high or the lowest low of the last x number of days.

The x is determined for each market based on the volatility characteristics of the market. What will work for one stock because of its volatility will not necessarily work for another stock. Ideal examples of the multigap buy and sell signals are shown, respectively, in Figures 5-13 and 5-14.

Holding Beyond the Day Time Frame (Exit on the _n_th Profitable Opening).   Sometimes it is more profitable to hold beyond the time

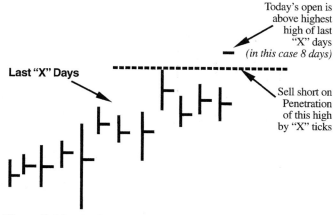

Figure 5-13.   Multigap sell signal.

frame of one day. A comparison of exit on the day of entry and exit beyond the entry day will give you an example of how the two procedures compare.

In some stocks, gap trades that show a poor record of success when closed out at the end of the day can improve dramatically using the multi-gap method. Take a little time to review this approach in a number of different markets and as described in the following section, "Rules of the Multigap Method." You may find it worth your while to pursue it.

Rules of the Multigap Method.   Following are some rules to keep in mind when using the multigap method:

- If a stock opens below its lowest low of the last x days, then buy on a penetration back up through the low by x ticks.
- If a stock opens above its highest high of the last x days, then sell short on a penetration back down through the high by x ticks.
- Exit on a predetermined risk management stop loss, on the close of the day, or on the nth profitable opening (to be defined subsequently).

Note that by x *days,* I mean a given number of days as defined for the indicated markets. The x days can be different for buy signals and for sell signals. The nth profitable opening is also determined by market. By a *profitable opening,* I mean an opening price that is above the buy price or below the sell short price.

You simply count the number of days in which the opening was profitable. Then on the nth profitable opening, you exit (unless you have been stopped out

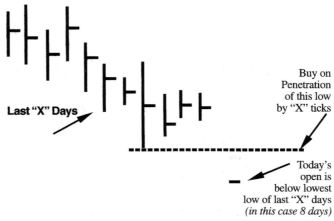

Figure 5-14.   Multigap buy signal.

first). See Figure 5-15 for a performance summary in Daily Yahoo! using multi-gap signals. Also see Figures 5-16 and 5-17 for more examples of this method.

This is a truly simple approach that I believe has considerable merit for position traders. You might want to take some time to evaluate this method. (See also Figures 5-18 and 5-19 for additional gap trade examples.)

In order to find the best fit for given stocks, you will need to adjust gap size and penetration size for each by using a back-testing approach. Hence, the results could be even better than what has been stated here. As you can see, this is an improvement on the basic gap method previously described.

Intraday Follow-up of Gap Trends

Finally, another aspect of the gap trade is the trailing stop loss. For those who are active day traders, a trailing stop loss method may be a valuable addition to the gap trade and/or the multigap trade. There are many different procedures you can use for the implementation of trailing stops. The most common is to set a *floor level* and a percentage trailing stop of the floor level.

In other words, if you enter a stock and set a floor level of $1000, this means that before you can begin using a trailing intraday stop loss, your position will need to show an open profit of $1000. As soon as this has happened, your trailing stop-loss percentage will kick in. Should your open profit decline by more than a given amount, you will be stopped out at your trailing stop loss.

```
jb.Gap System  YHOO-Daily    04/12/1996 - 02/07/2000

                    Performance Summary:  All Trades

   Total net profit      $ 290131.50   Open position P/L      $    3499.50
   Gross profit          $ 448078.50   Gross loss             $-157947.00

   Total # of trades            75     Percent profitable           68%
   Number winning trades        51     Number losing trades         24

   Largest winning trade $  98706.00   Largest losing trade   $  -11075.00
   Average winning trade $   8785.85   Average losing trade   $   -6581.13
   Ratio avg win/avg loss     1.34     Avg trade(win & loss)  $    3868.42

   Max consec. winners          10     Max consec. losers            2
   Avg # bars in winners         9     Avg # bars in losers          7

   Max intraday drawdown $ -31389.50
   Profit factor               2.84    Max # contracts held          1
   Account size required $  31389.50   Return on account          924%
```

Figure 5-15. Gap signals/Yahoo! performance summary. Note that this gap method holds beyond the daily time frame.

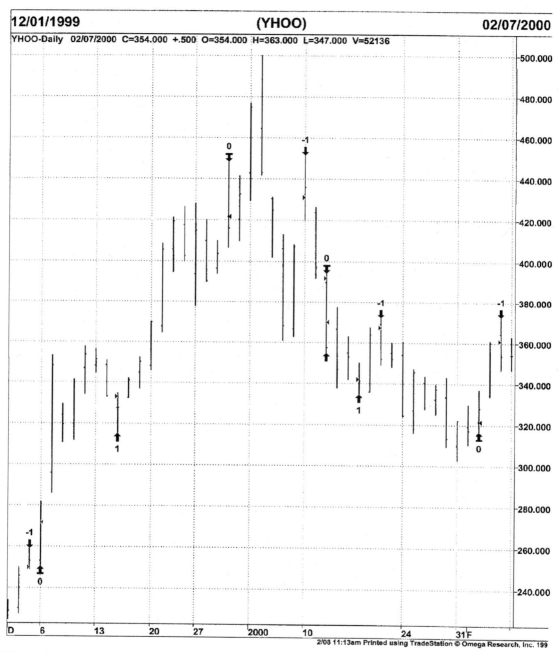

Figure 5-16.   Multigap buy and sell signals on a Yahoo! Inc. chart. 1 = buy signal; −1 = sell short signal; 0 = exit on stop loss.

```
jb.Gap System  First Data Corp. - NYSE-Daily
          04/21/1994 - 03/20/2000
        Performance Summary:  All Trades
```

Total net profit	$28911.50	Open position P/L	-$1062.50
Gross profit	$30486.50	Gross loss	-$1575.00
Total # of trades	17	Percent profitable	94%
Number winning trades	16	Number losing trades	1
Largest winning trade	$4487.50	Largest losing trade	-$1575.00
Average winning trade	$1905.41	Average losing trade	-$1575.00
Ratio avg win/avg loss	1.21	Avg trade(win & loss)	$1700.68
Max consec. winners	9	Max consec. losers	1
Avg # bars in winners	39	Avg # bars in losers	30
Max intraday drawdown	-$6906.50		
Profit factor	19.36	Max # contracts held	1
Account size required	$6906.50	Return on account	419%

```
        Performance Summary: Long Trades
```

Total net profit	$13924.00	Open position P/L	$1062.50
Gross profit	$15499.00	Gross loss	-$1575.00
Total # of trades	11	Percent profitable	91%
Number winning trades	10	Number losing trades	1
Largest winning trade	$3175.00	Largest losing trade	-$1575.00
Average winning trade	$1549.90	Average losing trade	-$1575.00
Ratio avg win/avg loss	0.98	Avg trade(win & loss)	$1265.82
Max consec. winners	6	Max consec. losers	1
Avg # bars in winners	48	Avg # bars in losers	30
Max intraday drawdown	-$6905.50		
Profit factor	9.84	Max # contracts held	1
Account size required	$6906.50	Return on account	202%

```
        Performance Summary: Short Trades
```

Total net profit	$14987.50	Open position P/L	$0.00
Gross profit	$14987.50	Gross loss	-$0.00
Total # of trades	6	Percent profitable	100%
Number winning trades	6	Number losing trades	0
Largest winning trade	$4487.50	Largest losing trade	-$0.00
Average winning trade	$2497.92	Average losing trade	-$0.00
Ratio avg win/avg loss	100.00	Avg trade(win & loss)	$2497.92
Max consec. winners	6	Max consec. losers	0
Avg # bars in winners	24	Avg # bars in losers	0
Max intraday drawdown	-$937.50		
Profit factor	100.00	Max # contracts held	1
Account size required	$937.50	Return on account	1599%

Figure 5-17. Multigap signals in First Data Corp. This summary shows multigap signals with the long entry gap as two days and the short entry gap as five days using an exit on the 25th profitable opening. Note that this is *not* a day-trading method. (Gap size = 3 ticks for long and short entry. Penetration size = 1 tick for long entry, 3 ticks for short entry.)

```
jb.Gap System  YHOO-Daily   04/12/1996 - 03/31/2000

                 Performance Summary:  All Trades

Total net profit      $   17293.50   Open position P/L    $       0.00
Gross profit          $   68574.00   Gross loss           $  -51280.50

Total # of trades           102      Percent profitable           69%
Number winning trades        70      Number losing trades         32

Largest winning trade $    6690.00   Largest losing trade $   -5475.00
Average winning trade $     979.63   Average losing trade $   -1602.52
Ratio avg win/avg loss       0.61    Avg trade(win & loss)$     169.54

Max consec. winners          25      Max consec. losers            7
Avg # bars in winners         2      Avg # bars in losers          4

Max intraday drawdown $  -15325.50
Profit factor                1.34    Max # contracts held          1
Account size required $   15325.50   Return on account          113%


                 Performance Summary:  Long Trades

Total net profit      $   24149.00   Open position P/L    $       0.00
Gross profit          $   47168.50   Gross loss           $  -23019.50

Total # of trades            57      Percent profitable           77%
Number winning trades        44      Number losing trades         13

Largest winning trade $    6690.00   Largest losing trade $   -5475.00
Average winning trade $    1072.01   Average losing trade $   -1770.73
Ratio avg win/avg loss       0.61    Avg trade(win & loss)$     423.67

Max consec. winners          21      Max consec. losers            6
Avg # bars in winners         2      Avg # bars in losers          4

Max intraday drawdown $   -6975.50
Profit factor                2.05    Max # contracts held          1
Account size required $    6975.50   Return on account          346%


                 Performance Summary:  Short Trades

Total net profit      $   -6855.50   Open position P/L    $       0.00
Gross profit          $   21405.50   Gross loss           $  -28261.00

Total # of trades            45      Percent profitable           58%
Number winning trades        26      Number losing trades         19

Largest winning trade $    3018.00   Largest losing trade $   -5475.00
Average winning trade $     823.29   Average losing trade $   -1487.42
Ratio avg win/avg loss       0.55    Avg trade(win & loss)$    -152.34

Max consec. winners          10      Max consec. losers            5
```

Figure 5-18.   Multiple-day gap signals in Yahoo! Inc.

Figure 5-19. Gap trades in PMC Sierra. B = buy gap; E = exit gap; S = sell gap; N = gap not filled; + = exit at a profit; – = exit at a loss; 0 = break even.

I find that this approach provides good protection for open day-trading profits. While it won't get you out of the trade at the maximum profit, it will give you some degree of profit protection. In using a trailing stop loss, make certain that your stop loss is not so close to the current price of the market that you'll get stopped out immediately. In other words, you need to give the market plenty of room to oscillate back and forth without stopping you out on what might be considered a random move in the price.

Summary

The basic gap trade is a viable method for day trading. The multigap trade has potential as well. Both approaches are specific, objective, and applicable to the day time frame. They can both be back-tested. The motivated trader will take a little time and effort to find the best combination of the major variables associated with both the gap trade and the multigap trade.

These variables are specifically: the length of days in gap window, the size of the opening gap, the size of the gap penetration, and the stop loss. Once a profit has been made, I suggest the use of a trailing stop loss. While the trailing stop loss may decrease accuracy slightly in some cases, there are markets in which accuracy increases, as well as average profit per trade. Your trailing stop loss should be large enough to allow for market movement without stopping you out on a random move. Note that I have also given you details on gap methods that hold trades beyond the day time frame and are therefore not day trading methods.

6

Intraday Application of Stochastics

The application of the stochastic indicator (SI), as originally developed by George Lane, has often been misunderstood and misused. This is unfortunate because the SI has excellent potential for day traders (as well as position traders). While the SI has long been touted by its proponents as the be-all and end-all of indicators, I do not see it as such.

The SI has its positive aspects as well as its limitations. It can be used in a variety of ways, some of which have good profit potential and others which are limited in their ability to produce viable results. This chapter will illustrate what I consider to be some of the more valuable applications of the SI for the purpose of day trading. I will provide specifics regarding SI applications, possible limitations, advantages, and expectations of the various methods.

Stochastics: Basic Explanation

The stochastic indicator consists of two values: percent K and percent D. Percent D is a derivative of percent K. Percent K is determined by using a simple mathematical formula. The first step in calculating the SI results in the *fast SI*. The fast SI is *slowed* by a moving average and called the *slow SI*.

We will be working with the slow stochastic indicator, so termed because it makes slower oscillations than the fast SI. The SI is a momentum-type indicator inasmuch as it compares prices in the present time frame with prices a given number of time frames back (i.e., weeks, days, hours, minutes). Once the values are determined, the SI can be used (or abused) in a variety of different ways.

The SI is one of the most popular contemporary indicators in the stock and futures markets. This, in and of itself, does not mean that the SI is the best indicator. On the contrary, it may very well mean that, as incorrectly used by many traders, the SI may be one of the worst indicators. However, I hasten to add that when applied consistently and with concise rules, the SI in its traditional applications can be a profitable indicator for day traders (and others as well).

What follows is a summary of the basic stochastic indicator, followed by some of the more traditional applications for day traders, as well as information on my stochastic pop (SP) method, which is, I believe, one of the more effective methods of day trading.

The Basic Stochastic Indicator

Futures traders have discovered through trial and error that effective timing indicators can be applied in many ways and in a variety of combinations with other indicators. Dr. George Lane advanced numerous applications for his stochastic indicator; I have, through persistence, considerable research, and the school of hard knocks, amplified on George Lane's original research. In fact, George has adapted at least one of my uses of stochastics—the stochastic pop indicator—to his own use.

Simply stated, the SI is a price oscillator, which compares today's price behavior with the price behavior x number of periods ago. A 14-day SI, for example, compares a derivative of today's price with a price 14 trading days ago. The raw stochastic number is converted to a percentage reading, smoothed, and then compared to a moving average of itself.

Hence, the SI consists of two numbers expressed as a percentage at each price bar. Since both lines are smoothed, and since one line, percent D, is a derivative of percent K (usually a three-period moving average of the first-line percent K), the visual effect is one which easily shows highs and lows in the SI correlated closely with highs and lows in price.

There are two forms of the SI: fast and slow. The fast SI consists of two lines which often gyrate wildly from low to high and back again; the slow

SI is a smoother version of the fast and moves more gradually from low to high and back again. There is a strong correlation between tops and bottoms in price and SI tops and bottoms. The SI is, therefore, a powerful indicator, which may be used by short-term, position, and day traders alike.

The important issue regarding the SI, whether fast or slow, is its method of application. As we will later see, there are numerous ways in which the SI may be used. It is the purpose of this chapter to provide you with what I believe are some of the more powerful methods for day traders. I am confident that those who understand and consistently apply the principles I am about to teach will appreciate both the simplicity and the power of these techniques.

Before introducing the basic approaches to SI timing, I'd like to stress the following important aspects of stochastics:

- *Many traders consider an SI of 75 percent or higher as an indication that a top is imminent, and a stochastic of 25 percent or lower is often considered a sign of an imminent bottom.*

- *The fact that the SI reaches an overbought condition (i.e., 75 percent or higher) or an oversold condition (25 percent or lower) does not necessarily indicate that action should be taken immediately.* This is the single most severe drawback of traditional stochastic implementation.

- *Many traders use the SI as a stand-alone system.* Although there is nothing wrong with this approach, I have found that with only a few exceptions the addition of timing indicators can improve overall results, regardless of which SI technique you are using.

Basic Approaches to SI Timing

Percent K and Percent D Crossover Signals. The stochastic indicator can be used in either its fast or its slow mode. As you know, the slow SI is a moving average version of the fast SI mode. I recommend using the slow SI, since the fast SI oscillates too wildly. One method of SI timing is to use the slow SI for buy and sell signals on crossovers of the percent K and the percent D SI lines.

This approach is illustrated in Figure 6-1. This application of the SI requires a considerable amount of trading, which varies directly with the length of the SI indicator. Shorter lengths of the SI result in more trades, and vice versa.

This technique is subject to the same limitations found in virtually all moving averages and oscillator applications: it generates numerous false signals and tends to give back too much in profits.

25 Percent and 75 Percent SI Crossovers.   Generally speaking, an SI reading of 75 percent or higher is considered overbought and a reading of 25 percent or lower is considered oversold. Because the SI can remain in the overbought (OB) or the oversold (OS) area for lengthy periods, we advise against sell decisions made simply on the basis of an OB condition or buy decisions made simply on the basis of an OS condition.

If you use the SI for the purpose of selling and buying on such extremes, you must wait for the cross to occur from OB back under 75 or for a cross above 25 from OS. This approach to the use of the SI requires you to wait for the SI to rise to 75 percent or higher and then fall below 75 percent on a closing basis; when it does, you will sell or reverse your long position to short.

Wait for the SI to fall to 25 percent or lower and then rise above 25 percent on a closing basis. When it does, you will buy or reverse your short position to the long side. This application of the SI has good potential for trading in virtually all time frames.

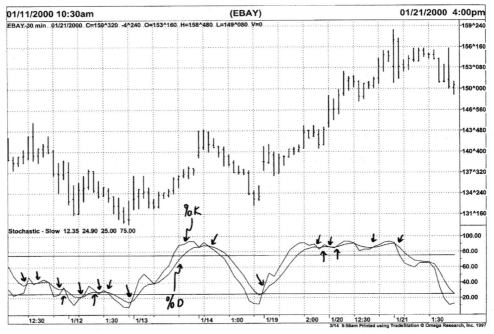

Figure 6-1. Slow stochastic 14-period on a 30-minute e-Bay with arrows showing percent K and D crossovers.

Remember, however, that the SI alone will not tell you where to put your stop or where to take your profit. You must use your other methods to do so or you must rely on your own judgment for stop-loss placement. As with any method or system, you must be prepared to take your losses when necessary.

Please don't resort to excuses to avoid taking your loss and don't add to a losing position just because the SI is heading in a given direction. The SI is not infallible. I have found, however, that when used in conjunction with the other timing signals, the SI achieves a greater degree of accuracy while limiting false signals and risk.

I have found the 75/25 approach to be more fruitful than the crossover method described in the previous section. The technique is very simple. Figures 6-2 and 6-3 illustrate this approach using 30-minute data. The 75/25 method may be used in virtually any time frame and will work well in 5-, 10-, or 15-minute charts.

It is also applicable to 30-minute data; however, when used on data longer than 20 minutes' duration, it no longer serves the purpose of day traders very well.

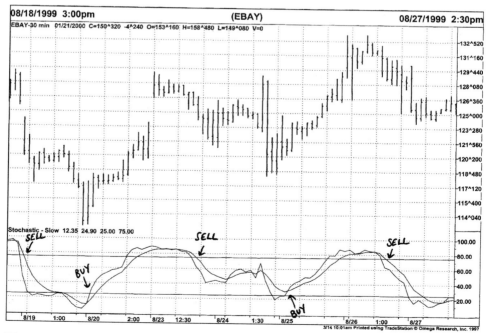

Figure 6-2. Thirty-minute eBay showing 75/25 crossover signals.

Intraday Stochastic Pop: Definition

I've been asked on many occasions why I call my unique use of stochastics the *stochastic pop* indicator (referred to hereafter as the SP). Very simply, the SP is so termed because *it enters markets when most traders consider markets to be overbought or oversold.*

In other words, the SP signals a buy when a market is considered by the vast majority of traders to be overbought and incapable of going any higher. The SP enters short positions when the majority of traders consider the market to be oversold and unlikely to go any lower. In other words, *I have found that markets tend to* pop *like a kernel of corn at the right temperature, once they reach certain levels on the SI.*

Through the years, I have found that the ideas of being overbought and oversold are fallacies. *The fact is that a market is never too overbought* to go higher and hardly ever too oversold to go lower. Since there is a natural limit on how low prices can go (i.e., zero), there does eventually come a point at which prices are ideally too low and oversold.

On the upside, however, as we have seen many times over the last 25 years, there is no limit to how high prices can go. Therefore, the SP method

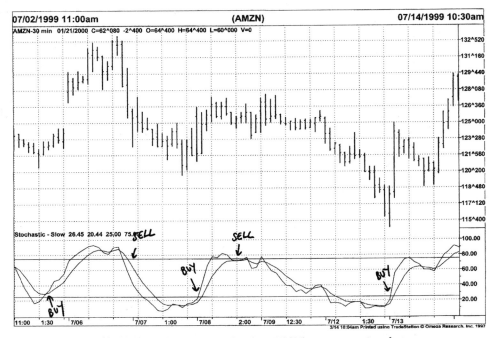

Figure 6-3. Thirty-minute Amazon.com showing 75/25 crossover signals.

takes advantage of market momentum by buying when momentum is strong and selling when momentum is weak in the expectation that the move will continue long enough to yield a profit.

In other words, the SP is, in a sense, consistent with the laws of physics, which state that a body in motion tends to stay in motion until it runs out of energy. In studying the stock and futures markets, I have found that many large moves occur quickly toward the end of a bullish trend and toward the end of a bearish trend. Frequently, the period of greatest upside momentum over the shortest period of time occurs after a market has become overbought and after a market has become oversold. The SP attempts to capitalize on this condition.

SP Parameters

Here are the rules of application for the SP. Using a 14-period slow stochastic indicator, a buy signal will be triggered when percent K is at 75 percent or higher at the end of the period you are using. For the purpose of day trading with the SP, I prefer either 5- or 10-minute data. Consequently, once the SI has closed at 75 percent or higher on percent K using 5- or 10-minute data, you will be buying immediately upon that 5- or 10-minute posting.

Your buy will always be at the market. From time to time there may be sufficient leeway to allow a specific price order; however, I leave that type of jockeying up to you, since it is not usually a simple matter. Once you have established your position, either use a risk management stop loss or exit your position at the market as soon as percent K and percent D have crossed one another at the end of your 5- or 10-minute segment.

See Figures 6-4, 6-5, and 6-6 for graphic explanation and illustrations of the SP method. Note that the following explanations are used on many of the charts in this chapter as well as in the chapters that follow:

B = Buy to establish new long position

S = Sell to establish new short position

SL = Close out long position and go flat

CS = Cover short positions and go flat

As you can see from a close examination of these figures, in every case that there was a buy or a sell SP signal, the results would have been profitable even after having been stopped out on the exit signal. Remember that once the exit signal has occurred you must exit your position at the market.

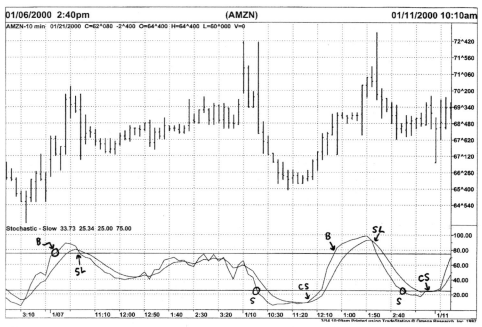

Figure 6-4. Stochastic pop signals on a 10-minute Amazon.com chart.

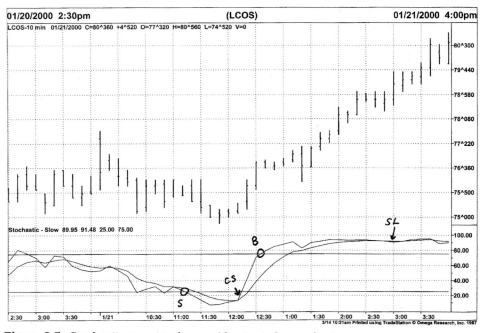

Figure 6-5. Stochastic pop signals on a 10-minute Lycos chart.

Assume now that once you have entered by SP and exited according to the rules, percent K declines under 75 percent and then in a future at the end of a subsequent 5- or 10-minute segment goes to 75 percent or higher. What to do? Simply enter a long position again and trade by the rules. You will find a number of such instances illustrated in Figures 6-7 and 6-8.

Although the SP technique is ultimately very simple, it does require close attention and you must, by all means, watch closely for those crossovers or you will lose money with this method. Before you attempt to implement this approach, take the time to follow it closely in actual market conditions so that you may test your knowledge and develop your skill with the SP method.

As you can see from the illustrations, the SP sell condition on an intra-day basis can also be used on 5- or 10-minute data; however, it sells once percent K falls below 25 percent after first having been above it. Price execution is at the market in all cases. But, as I've said earlier, you might decide to attempt specific price orders if you'd like to take the chance. Exit of the SP sell will be at the market once percent K and percent D have crossed.

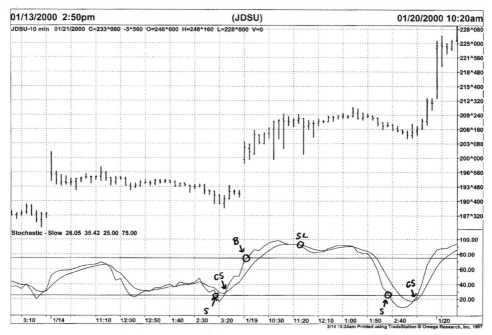

Figure 6-6. Stochastic pop signals on a 10-minute JDS Uniphase chart.

In any event, do remember that the SP intraday method is merely a day-trading method. I recommend against carrying a position beyond the end of the day.

Stocks in Which the SP Works Well

In my experience, the SP on an intraday basis works well in highly volatile stocks—currently this includes many of the NASDAQ stocks. Naturally, this may change over time. Currently technology stocks are among the best day-trading vehicles. High-volatility and high-volume stocks will be your best bet. These will be your best trading vehicles for this and many other methods discussed in this book.

Hit-and-Run Trading Using the SP

One of the characteristics of the SP method is that it lends itself readily to the application of my "hit-and-run" technique. What this amounts to is simply entering a long or a short position, consistent with the signals,

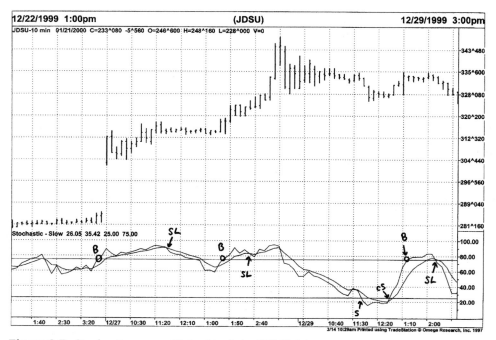

Figure 6-7. Stochastic pop multiple signals in JDS Uniphase.

at the market in order to grab a quick profit on the long or short side. Of course, the advantage in so doing is that you will take many quick profits. The disadvantage is that you will sacrifice larger moves, which may occur once you have exited the position.

In order to have the best of all possible worlds, I suggest trading larger positions. Here's how it would work in practice. Assume that an SP buy signal has occurred. Instead of trading just 100 shares, you trade several hundred shares. As soon as the stock has moved in your favor by a predetermined amount, you exit part of the position. You hold the remaining shares according to the rules. In so doing, you will trade several hundred shares for hit and run; the other you will trade according to the rules.

If, however, you did not exit when the percent K and percent D lines crossed but rather maintained your position, the potential profit would have been significantly greater. This is a more aggressive method because it allows you to hold your original SP position for a longer period of time. *To exit the position, use a close trailing stop, which will follow up your position, preferably every half hour or more frequently, in order to lock in your profit and protect you in the event of a quick reversal in trend.*

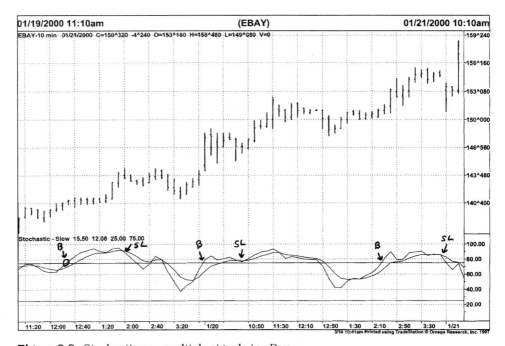

Figure 6-8. Stochastic pop multiple signals in eBay.

What You Can Expect

The SP technique has been back-tested extensively on historical data. Using various combinations of percentages to trigger SP entry (i.e., 75 percent, 65 percent, 60 percent for buying; 30 percent, 25 percent, 15 percent for selling), I have found that the accuracy of SP in terms of follow-through in the direction of the signal is fairly high.

Even in a large sample size such as the one I tested, accuracy as high as 65 percent in terms of follow-through in the direction of the signal was not uncommon during certain time frames.

Note however that, as with most day-trading methods, you will need to be highly selective about the stocks you trade, quick to enter and exit, and highly disciplined in limiting losses. Do not expect immediate results and avoid low-volatility stocks.

Summary

This chapter addressed several applications for the implementation of stochastics as applied to day trading. Overall I believe that, when used in the fashion described by the methods discussed in this chapter, the SI can give the day trader a distinct advantage.

$$7$$

The Open Versus Close
Oscillator

*And when you know what not to do in order to
not lose money, you learn what to do in order
to win . . .*

EDWIN LEFEBVRE

One of the most important relationships in the stock and commodity markets is that of the opening versus the closing price of the day. Note that this relationship as I use it applies only to the day session trading and *not* to after-hours trading. Several day-trading systems and methods have been developed based on this relationship for application.

Oscillator Defined

An oscillator is a timing indicator that comprises two or more moving averages. To *oscillate* means to move back and forth between extremes. An oscillator, therefore, is an indicator that changes values between two extreme levels. The stochastic indicator (Chapter 4) is an oscillator, and so are the relative strength index (RSI), the momentum (MOM), and the rate of change (ROC). Not all oscillators are the same, even though they are based on the same general idea.

The basic construction of a two-line oscillator appears as shown in Figure 7-1. As you can see, the oscillator values generate buy and sell signals when they change their positions by crossing one another. The simplest oscillator consists of two moving averages. Typically, when a fast MA crosses above or below a slow MA, signals to buy or sell are generated.

Such indicators as moving average convergence/divergence (MACD) consist of exponential moving averages which generate buy and sell signals when they cross, very similar to the relationships shown in Figure 7-1. The MACD is a two-line indicator.

The crossings of the lines generate buy and sell signals, as I have marked accordingly on Figure 7-1. In most cases, follow-through in the direction of the crossover occurs and is frequently substantial. Accordingly, the MACD is a valid method for use in stock day trading. The MACD is not a perfect indicator, yet it does alert us to changes in market direction within its defined time frame.

Figure 7-2 illustrates how MACD buy and sell signals appear on a 60-minute Commerce One chart. You will note that the MACD on Figure 7-1 is

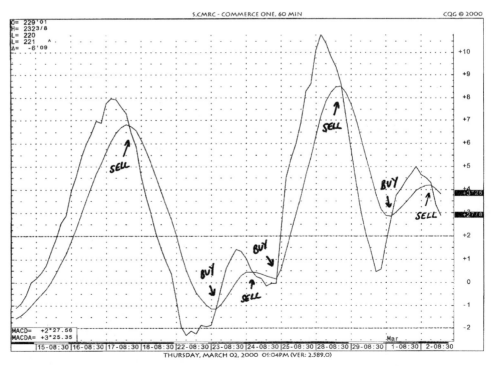

Figure 7-1. Ideal MACD oscillator signals on 60-minute Commerce One chart.

the same as the MACD on Figure 7-2; however, Figure 7-2 also shows the price.

With respect to price, a short position would have been established initially at 188 after a large move up was closed out. The next signal was a buy to cover the short and a reversal to long at about 180. The method then reversed to a sell at 178 and a buy at about 179. A large move up followed, with profit taken at about 211, where a short position was established. The short was then closed at 221 and, at the far right on the chart, the last long position from 222 was reversed to short. Note that these figures are approximate.

Figure 7-3 also shows MACD buy and sell signals on a 30-minute Verio chart. As you can see, the MACD is an outstanding indicator for trading such moves.

In spite of the fact that the MACD is an effective technique for stock day trading, there is another oscillator method that I feel has more potential for the day trader. The MACD, in my experience, is a very effective method for

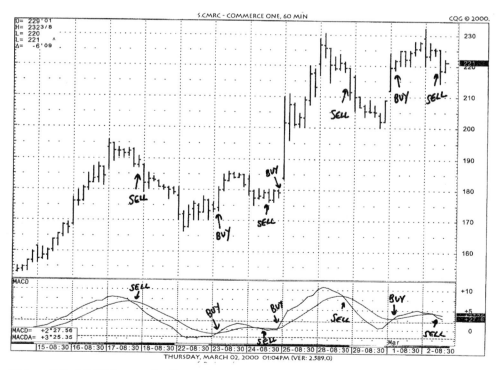

Figure 7-2. MACD buy and sell signals on a 60-minute Commerce One chart.

trading short-term price swings of from two to six days' duration. Yet, an oscillator based on the open versus close relationship appears to be more quickly responsive to changes in stock trends.

Definition

The opening price of a stock is defined, for our purposes, as the first price of a given time segment.

Opens Versus Closes

Although there is no such thing as a 5-minute open or a 5-minute close, we will define the first price of a 5-minute time segment as the *open* and the last price of the 5-minute bar as the *close*.

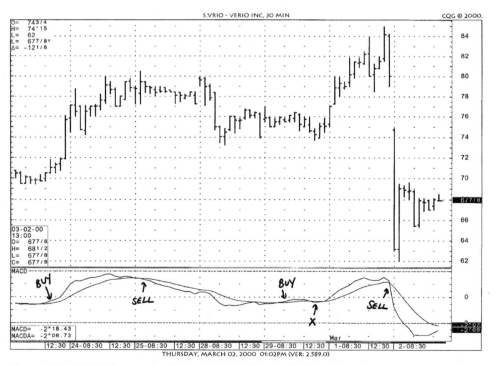

Figure 7-3. MACD buy and sell signals on a 30-minute Verio Inc. chart.

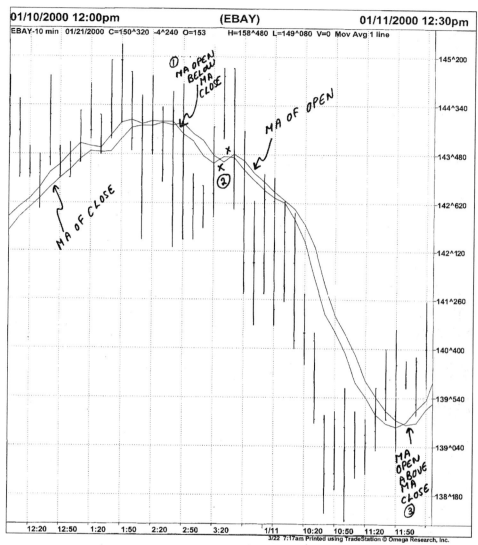

Figure 7-4. Ideal O/C oscillator signals on a 10-minute eBay chart. This figure shows the open and close MAs (marked accordingly on the 10-minute eBay chart). You will note that at the point marked 1, the MA of the open drops below the MA of the close. This constitutes a sell signal. At point 2, which I have marked with 2 Xs, the lines cross again but only for one posting. As you will see later in this chapter, two consecutive postings are necessary in order to generate a signal. At point 3, the lines cross again, this time generating a buy signal.

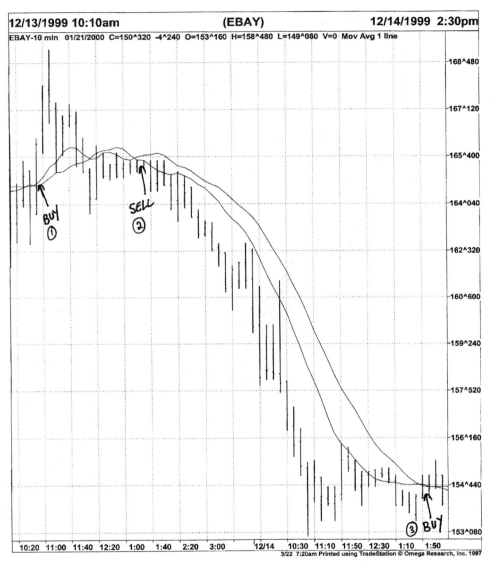

Figure 7-5. Open and close oscillator signals on a 10-minute eBay chart. This figure shows a buy signal at point 1, followed by a sell signal at point 2, subsequent to which a large decline developed. The decline continued into the next day (14 December 1999) until a buy signal occurred at point 3.

Figure 7-6. Open and close oscillator signals on a 10-minute AOL chart. Sell and buy signals have been marked correspondingly. As a practical consideration you must remember that day trades will need to be closed out at the end of the day. Accordingly, you will exit your position at the end of the day and reinstate it the next day, consistent with the existing signal. (I also have shown these entries and exits on Figures 7-8 through 7-12.)

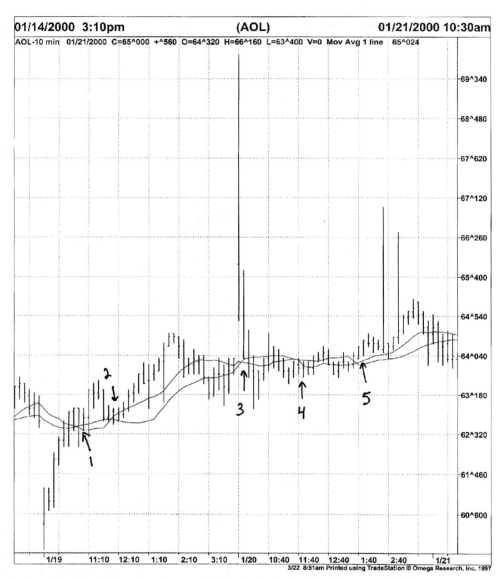

Figure 7-7. O/C false signals on a 10-minute AOL chart. This figure illustrates numerous false signals. Either changing the MA lengths and/or requiring a larger magnitude of crossover can eliminate these false signals. As a point of information, those who seek to use this method in ultra-short-term trading (often called *scalping*—a politically incorrect term these days) will observe that once a crossover has occurred there is typically follow-through in the direction of the signal. Traders who are nimble could quickly grab a profit and wait for the next signal. The points numbered 1 through 5 on this chart clearly show this type of follow-through on a very short-term basis.

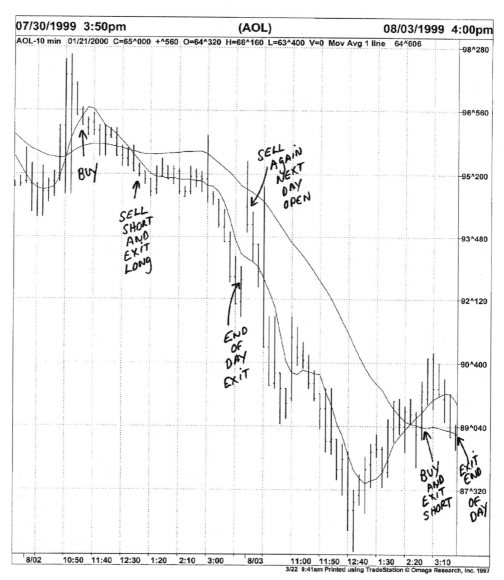

Figure 7-8. O/C signals on 10-minute data.

The relationship is a simple one. It is based on the well-established pattern for closing prices in a bull trend to be higher than opening prices and for closing prices in a bear trend to be lower than opening prices. By comparing a moving average of the 5-, 10-, or 15-minute openings with a moving average of the 5-, 10-, or 15-minute closings, we can quickly detect trend changes either before they occur or very early in their inception.

Figures 7-4 and 7-5 illustrate the ideal signals and relationship to which I am referring, using a 10-minute chart of eBay. Examine my buy and sell signals in relation to price trend changes during the day. Figure 7-6 shows the same oscillator combination and signals on an AOL 10-minute chart.

As you can see from the illustrations, the signals are very reliable and tend to signal major moves. I call this method the O/C oscillator. Although the O/C method is wonderful for catching large intraday price swings, it does have its limitations, which I will discuss later. Before doing so, however, I'll review the construction of the O/C oscillator and then I'll give you the rules for using it.

Figure 7-9. O/C signals on a 10-minute Exodus Communications chart.

Note that the O/C MA as shown in Figures 7-4 and 7-5 uses a simple MA. To achieve a better result, we use a smoothed MA. Also, we can express the OC/MA as one line by subtracting one MA from the other, thus generating signals when the single line crosses above and below zero.

Construction of the O/C for Day Trading in Stocks

The O/C is constructed as follows:

1. *Use two smoothed moving averages (MAs) as follows:*

   a. A smoothed moving average of the opening prices consisting of 6 to 10 periods on 5-, 10-, 15-, or 20-minute data.

   b. A second smoothed moving average, which consists of closing prices of 12 to 24 periods on 5-, 10-, 15-, or 20-minute data.

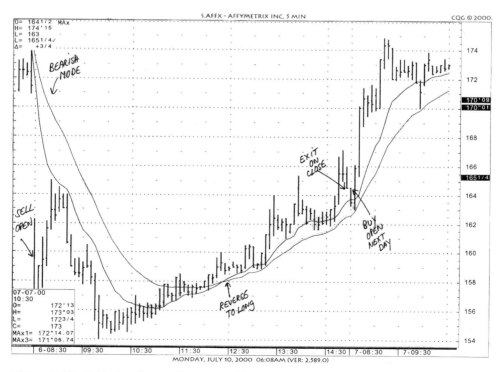

Figure 7-10. O/C signals on a 5-minute Affymetrix Inc. chart.

2. *Buy and sell on crossovers of the two MA lines.* When the MA of the close crosses over the MA of the open, a buy is signaled, and when the MA of the close falls below the MA of the open, a sell is signaled.

3. *You will need to adjust the lengths used as a function of the time span and the stock(s) you are trading* (i.e., 5-, 10-, 15-, or 20-minute data). There are no hard-and-fast rules for doing this.

   You will need to use your judgment; however, after you work with this method for a while you will become quite adept at making the proper selections. (The formula for smoothed MA is in the Glossary of Day-Trading Terms at the end of this book.)

4. *An important issue, which you will need to deal with, is the amount of the crossover.* In other words, you will need to determine how much of a crossover will be sufficient to generate a signal in either direction. In this respect, consider Figure 7-7. As you can see, the minor crossovers that do occur are not reliable. They must be sufficiently large. You will need to

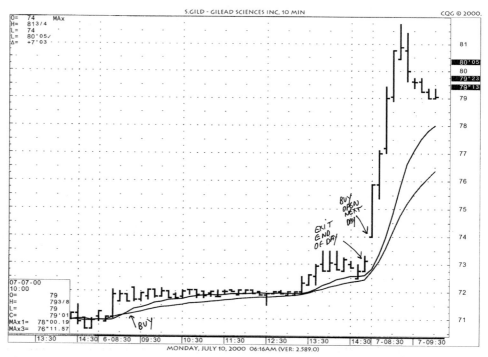

Figure 7-11. O/C signals on a 10-minute Gilead Sciences chart.

determine the crossover amount or threshold. You can do this fairly easily by examining recent signals. Be sure to monitor the O/C performance closely.

5. *You may use O/C signals in the opposite direction to reverse positions, or you may use a trailing stop loss to exit prior to a reversing signal.* Some subjective decisions may be necessary in exiting trades that are initiated using O/C signals, but I stress that this is not a totally mechanical system. It does require decisions. It is, however, one of the most sensitive methods I have developed for day trading volatile stocks. Naturally, you will want to be out of all trades by the end of the day, and you will wait for the next day to enter on new signals.

Note also that it is important to require crossovers to occur on two consecutive postings (i.e., the time frame before a signal can be generated). This requirement reduces the number of false signals.

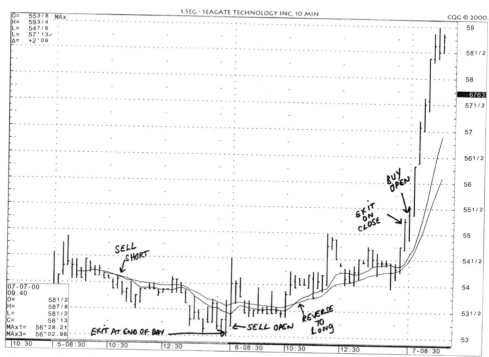

Figure 7-12. O/C signals on a 10-minute Seagate Technology chart.

Examining Some Signals

Figures 7-8 through 7-12 illustrate O/C signals in a number of stocks using various time lengths (along with my handwritten comments).

Summary

The O/C system is a sound and useful one for day traders. Its rules of application for entry signals are specific, objective, and mechanical. It is readily tracked by computer and tends to get on board when major moves occur within the day time frame. I recommend tracking this method in the more active markets, particularly those markets that have a high dollar value per tick.

As with most day-trade systems discussed in this book, entry signals are specific and objective. Exiting positions, however, are less objective. This method, in particular, is amenable to the use of a fairly close trailing stop loss. You may wish to exit at a given price or time target. It is not uncommon for large profits to be diminished substantially as a result of waiting for a reversing signal.

Yet another suggested method of exit is to use a shorter-term time frame for exit than was originally used for entry. If you use an entry signal generated on a 10-minute chart for a given stock, you could exit when the 3- or 5-minute chart for that stock gave its subsequent reversal signal. At this point you would not reverse position, you would merely close the position out. This, by the way, is an excellent method for exiting positions using timing signals other than the O/C.

8

One-Hour Breakout (OHB)

*. . . man must, as a simple survival strategy,
become aware of what is happening to him,
despite the attendant pain of such
comprehension . . .*

MARSHALL McLUHAN

Perhaps one of the most interesting and intriguing day-trading methods is what I call *one-hour breakout* (OHB). This is a method that I first developed in the late 1970s. It is both simple and easily applied, yet it is demanding inasmuch as it requires the trader to be present throughout the day, tracking prices every hour. This is why the method may not be suitable for all traders.

The OHB method has remained virtually unchanged since it was developed. This is a strong testimonial to its efficacy. I caution you, however, to remember that the OHB is a method, not a system, although it is systematic and has the potential to be used as a system. The OHB is designed to spot intraday price moves based on the five-minute closing prices during the first hour of the trading day.

Basic OHB Signals and Parameters

The basic methodology and operational procedures for using OHB measures are as follows:

■ *Plot the five-minute closing prices for the first hour of trading regardless of market* (see exceptions later on). By five-minute closing prices, I mean the

133

price at the end of every five minutes. The price used is the last price, not the intraday high or low price.

The ideal sell signal will look like Figures 8-1 and 8-2. Figures 8-3 and 8-4 show ideal buy signals.

Remember this—it is important: Use the price at the end of each five-minute period, not the high or low, but the last price for each five-minute period.

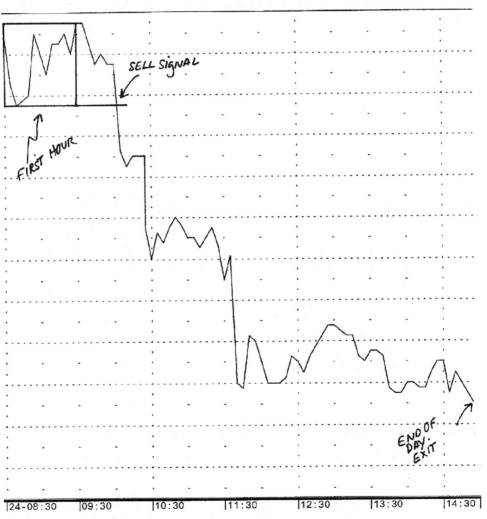

Figure 8-1. Ideal sell signal.

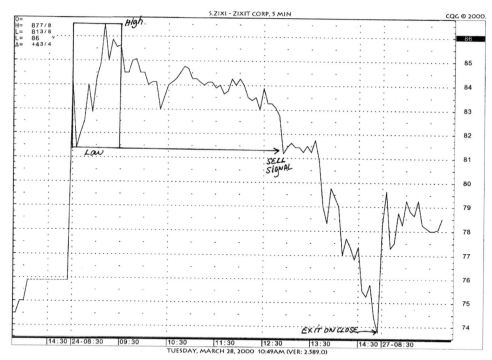

Figure 8-2. Sell signal in Zixit Corp.

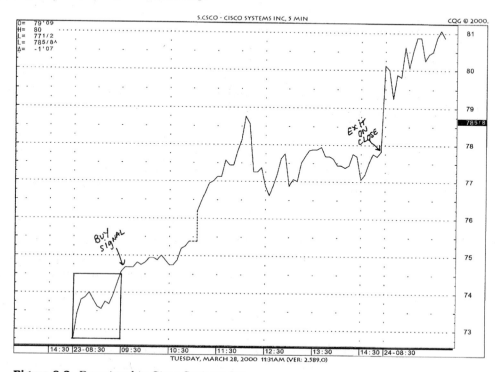

Figure 8-3. Buy signal in Cisco Systems Inc.

135

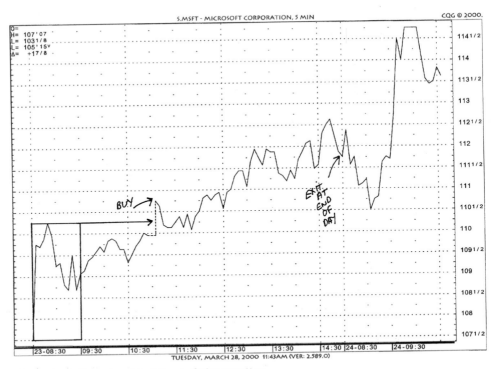

S.MSFT - MICROSOFT CORPORATION, 5 MIN   CQG © 2000.

Figure 8-4. Buy signal in Microsoft Corporation.

Once the first hour of five-minute closing price data has been gathered, the highest price will be used as a buying breakout point, whereas the lowest price will be used as a selling breakout point.

- *An upper breakout and* buy signal *will occur when prices have had a five-minute "close"* (i.e., plot) above the highest five-minute closing plot established during the first hour. You will then buy at the market using a five-minute closing stop loss below the lowest closing five-minute plot of the first hour.

- *A lower breakout and* sell signal *will occur when prices have had a five-minute close* (i.e., plot) below the lowest five-minute closing plot established during the first hour. You will then sell at the market using a five-minute closing stop loss above the highest closing five-minute plot of the first hour.

- *You will use a trailing stop loss that consists of a five-minute close below the lowest five-minute close of each previous hour for longs and above the highest five-minute close of the previous hour for short positions.*

- *As an alternative, you can use either a money management stop loss or a stop loss based on other indicators discussed in this book (i.e., moving averages or oscillators).*

- *You will exit positions by the end of the day or by being stopped out either at a loss or at your trailing stop loss for a profit.*

Tips and Suggestions for Using the OHB

- *The OHB method is best used in active markets, which tend to make large moves during the day.* Currently, stocks priced over $40 per share and higher, with about a million shares average daily trading volume, show the best potential for using this method.

- *Once you have established your position, be sure to use a trailing stop loss, or you may find your profit diminishing.* The whole idea of OHB trading is to grab profits, yet at the same time to give the market you are trading sufficient room to continue its move.

- *You may want to experiment with different time frames.* Study the markets you are trading for unique characteristics that allow short or long time windows to work better.

- *Multiple shares can offer you the best of possible worlds using the OHB.* If, for example, you enter your initial position with two hundred shares, then you can close one hundred shares out at a profit when the market either bulges or drops sharply and hold the remaining unit according to the rules, in the event that a further move is coming.

- *Trailing stop losses can and do work with the OHB.* Experiment with different stop-loss methods—in particular, with those described in this book.

- *Remember that the OHB can give two signals each day, a buy and a sell, or it may, on occasion, give no signals whatsoever.*

Summary

This chapter discussed and explained, in detail, the one-hour breakout method. This method was originally developed for day trading commodity futures markets. However, it has been adapted in this chapter for day trading volatility stocks.

As a mechanical trading method, the OHB has great potential, provided you use it consistently according to the rules. Because some of the market moves, subsequent trading signals can be quite volatile, this is a method that must be closely monitored by using live quotes. Delayed quotes will not suffice.

9

Computerized Short-Term Trading with Support and Resistance

Beware that you do not lose the substance by grasping at the shadow.

AESOP

Perhaps one of the most effective ways to trade for the short term is by using support and resistance methods. The various ways of using support and resistance all involve an essentially similar approach. The approach consists of two aspects. The first aspect requires an evaluation of the current *trend*, while the second aspect involves the determination of support and resistance.

In a market that is in an uptrend, the day trader will want to buy at support (as defined). In a market that is in a downtrend, the short-term trader will want to go short at resistance. These procedures are self-evident. The key issues here are severalfold, as follows:

■ How is the trend determined?

■ How can the short-term trader know when the trend is changing?

■ How can support be objectively determined in an uptrend?

■ How can resistance be objectively determined in a downtrend?

■ How can the short-term trader know when the market is essentially trendless and thereby not suitable for short-term trading using support and resistance methods?

The Traditional Method

The traditional method for determining support, resistance, and trend was for many years the domain of the chartist. Using methods that had been developed over the course of many years, the chartist employed paper charts, either hand-drawn or commercially published, to find a variety of chart patterns that purportedly would give clues to the trader as to market direction, strength, weakness and potential changes in trend, and support and resistance.

While these methods had their heyday in the 1950s through as late as the mid-1980s, the growth of day trading and the growth of computerized day trading have given rise to a host of mathematical models that appear to give better results. Furthermore, the methods of old are more subject to interpretation than are the more operationalized methods in use today. Bear in mind that there are still many E-traders who find the traditional methods helpful and who use them daily.

Most trading software programs contain tools that allow the user to draw and highlight various chart formations. These methods are not discussed here, inasmuch as *they are subject to individual interpretation and, therefore, not easily taught.* They are perhaps as much art as they are science. Several traders looking at the same information could easily reach several different conclusions.

However, the methods discussed in this chapter are primarily objective and are easily defined in operational terms so that they may be readily duplicated by other traders. While objectivity does not necessarily lead to profits or to 100 percent agreement among traders, it does go a long way toward formalizing procedures. And formalized procedures will be reproducible, as well as ultimately profitable, providing that the underlying assumptions of the approach are correct.

Determining the Trend

The first issue that confronts the short-term E-trader, whether in stocks or in commodities, is to determine the existing trend. There are many methods for doing so. Ultimately, traders will have their pet methods; however, it is not the method so much as how it is used that is important in the final analysis. I could write an entire book on methods that are valid approaches for determining trends and changes in trends.

This book, however, discusses only those that I believe have better potential for profit in short-term time frames. Note that the indicators discussed are my favorites, but they are certainly not the only ones you can employ for the purpose of determining trends and trend changes. You could, in fact, use virtually any method that is sensitive enough to detect a change in the intraday trend as well as reliable enough to correctly define the trend as either up, down, or sideways.

For the purpose of this approach, the trend is defined by using a 14-period momentum. If momentum is positive and has been so *for at least two consecutive postings*, then the trend is defined as up. If momentum is negative and has been so *for at least two consecutive postings*, then the trend is defined as down.

Once the trend has been so defined, we can employ support and resistance as the buy and sell method. Figure 9-1 shows a 60-minute Global Crossings Ltd. chart with the MAC indicator, and Figure 9-2 shows the MAC indicator on a 20-minute JDS Uniphase Corp. chart.

After the Trend Has Been Defined

One of the best ways for a day trader to capture profits is by trading with the ultra-short-term trend. There are various and sundry ways in which this

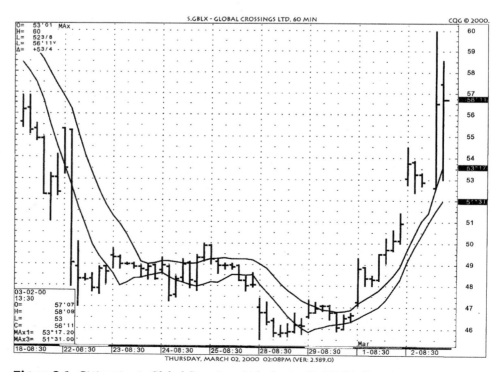

Figure 9-1. Sixty-minute Global Crossings Ltd. chart with MAC indicator.

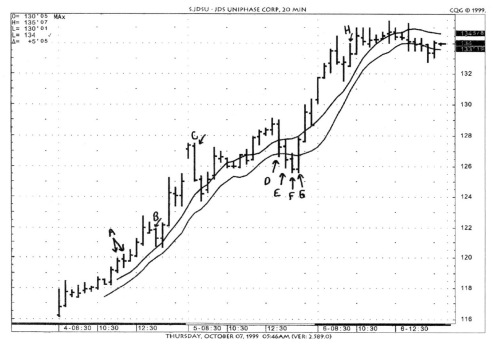

Figure 9-2. Twenty-minute JDS Uniphase Corp. chart with MAC signals.

can be achieved. My preferred method is to use the 3/3-channel method. The logic and methodology are simple and precise. I prefer this approach to the use of the MAC.

Once the trend has been defined, there are essentially two issues. The first issue is whether to take a position using timing alone (i.e., the cross above or below zero) or to take a position based on a support and resistance method. In actuality, both methods could be employed; however, if the trader wishes to use only support and resistance, then the crossing of momentum above or below zero will be only the first step in the procedure.

The next step is to define support and/or resistance levels. The method I prefer for this purpose is to use a moving average of lows for support and a moving average of highs for determining resistance.

Remember that *in order to use this method, there must be sufficient market volatility to make the game worthwhile.* There are many stocks that make large enough intraday moves to allow for sufficient profit potential in trading support and resistance methods on an intraday basis. And this is one of the reasons that many traders have been attracted to stocks for the purpose of day trading.

The 3/3 High/Low Channel

My recommendation to the computerized short-term trader is to use a three-period intraday moving average of the high and the low (easily available on most trading software). The rules of application are simple. Remember that the *shorter* the time frame you use (i.e., 50-minute, 20-minute, 10-minute), the *more* signals you will get and the *smaller* the price moves will be.

Your job is to determine the optimum frame as a function of market volatility. The moving average length I recommend is three units of the high and three units of the low. To some traders this will be reminiscent of my 10/8 moving average channel, but I assure you it is very different in its application. Figure 9-3 illustrates the 3/3 channel on an intraday chart showing support and resistance.

By way of introduction, however, here is a general description of the approach.

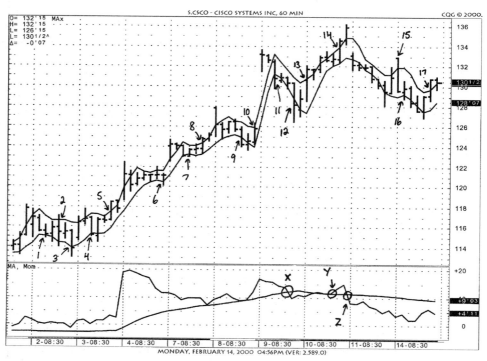

Figure 9-3. Support and resistance using the 3/3 high-low channel on a 60-minute Cisco Systems, Inc., chart. Points 2, 5, 8, 10, 13, 14, 15, and 17 show tests of resistance. Points 3, 4, 6, 7, 9, 11, 12, and 16 show tests of support. X and Y are buy signals. Z is a sell signal.

- The existing trend is determined by using the momentum/moving average as an indicator.

- As long as the 28-period momentum (MOM) remains above its moving average (MA), we assume the existing trend to be up. If the MOM falls below its MA, then we assume the trend is down.

- For support and resistance we use the 3 high/3 low MA channel.

- If the trend is defined as up, then we *buy* at the 3MA of the low and take profit at the 3MA of the high. (See Figure 9-3.)

- If the trend is defined as down, then we *sell short* at the 3MA of the high and take profit at the 3MA of the low. (See Figure 9-3.)

- We can use a multiple-share approach to ride the trades for bigger moves.

- We can hold through the end of the day rather than exit at support or resistance.

Details are described as follows.

- *The essence of the 3/3 approach is that it is more of a method than a system.* In other words, although it is a systematic approach, it does require some degree of judgment that is not totally mechanical. There are a few caveats that must be mentioned in conjunction with this approach. They concern the vital issues of risk and position size. While some of the caveats are general and applicable to all day-trading methods, some are unique to the 3/3 method. Note the following.

- *The 3/3 method works best in higher-priced stocks where the intraday moves are larger.*

- *The fact that 3/3 works best in such stocks* does not *preclude you from using it on lower- or medium-range-priced stocks if you want to take a larger position.* This is perfectly acceptable as long as you are comfortable with the method.

- *Sudden price reversals against you can occur in the event of unexpected news or market swings.* This is why it's necessary to use a stop or fail-safe approach with the 3/3. You will need to limit your losses (as you would need to do with all approaches). No matter how well 3/3 works for you, the fact remains that a stop loss is necessary. A strong string of 10 winning trades in a row can be erased by one large loss.

- *You will need to be very attentive to placing price orders every time your data updates.* If you are using the 3/3 with an hourly chart, then you'll have to place new orders every hour as soon as your new data posts. As you can see, the 3/3 is a method that requires you to be attentive and organized.

- *If you have trading software that will allow you to monitor the 3/3 in a number of different stocks, try to avoid using 3/3 in too many stocks of the same industry group.* In other words, you will want to diversify. Pick one or two stocks from several different categories in order to avoid excessive duplication.

- *3/3 works best in active stocks. Avoid stocks that have light trading volume.* You can spot such stocks by looking at either the actual trading volume in shares or the tick volume, or if you do not have access to these you can tell simply by looking at the price chart whether there is sufficient trading volume. A chart that is spotty or has very small hourly or 30-minute trading ranges indicates a stock that is too thinly traded. (See Figure 9-4 for an example.)

- *Since the 3/3 is a day-trading method, I suggest you avoid carrying positions overnight.* While I have described a method by which you can hold a stock for a longer move, the danger of a large opening move against you the

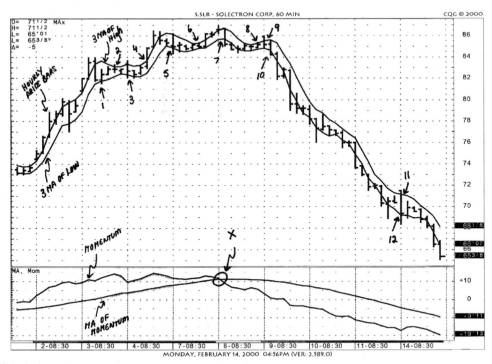

Figure 9-4. Sixty-minute Solectron Corporation chart showing 3/3 MA and MOM/MA signals. Sell at resistance to take profits at points 2, 4, and 6. Buy at support points 1, 3, 5, and 7. Sell short after bearish crossover X at points 8, 9, and 11. Buy back shorts at points 10 and 12.

next morning goes with the territory of holding beyond the day time frame.

- *While you can enter orders for the 3/3 in* after-hours *trading, this can be problematic,* inasmuch as trading volume tends to be light and you may have difficulty entering and/or exiting trades.
- *Finally, I strongly suggest that you take your time with the 3/3. Become totally familiar with it.* Test different time frames. Construct hypothetical scenarios and back-tests with your favorite trading stocks in order to see if the method is right for you.

The rules are as follows:

- If momentum has been above the zero line for at least two postings, then the trend is considered up.
- If the trend is up, then buy at support.
- Support is defined as the three-period moving average of lows.

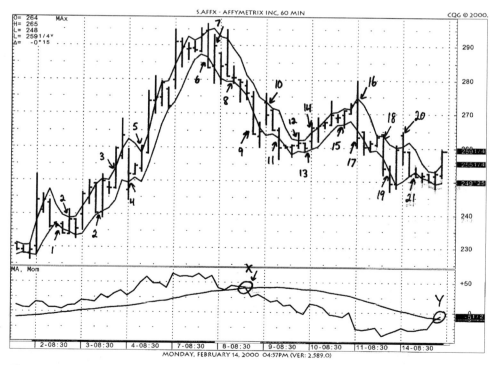

Figure 9-5. Sixty-minute Affymetrix Inc. chart showing 3/3 and MOM/MA signals. Trend is bullish at Y. Points 1 to 21 are buy or sell points consistent with momentum/MA trend.

- If you buy at support, take profit at resistance.
- Use a stop loss that is 100 percent of the average of the last three trading ranges—close only.
- Resistance is defined as the three-period moving average of the highs.
- If you buy at support and exit at resistance and the trend as defined is still up, then place another order to buy at support and repeat the same procedure.
- Do the opposite for sell signals.
- Do not trade signals that occur too close to the end of the trading day, since there will not be enough time for a profit to be made.
- Be out of all trades by the end of the day—win, lose, or draw.

As noted, longer time frames give larger moves and fewer trades. Figures 9-5 and 9-6 show how this method works. I have marked support, resistance, entries, and exits accordingly.

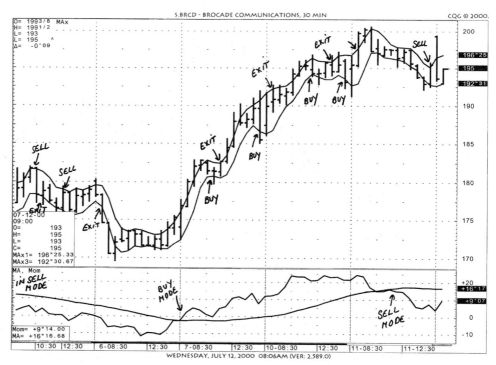

Figure 9-6. Five-minute Yahoo! Inc. chart showing momentum.

Summary

The use of momentum or momentum/moving average (MOM/MA) for determining trend and the use of the 3/3 channel can be an effective method for intraday trading in stocks. This chapter outlined the methodology, provided some specific examples, and listed a few caveats that must be considered when trading this approach.

Due to its intensive nature, it is a method that is well suited for the computerized day trader since numerous trades and signals are possible during any given day. The art behind the science is to have enough day trades to yield a profit but not so many as to result in more heat than light.

10
Grabbing Small but Consistent Intraday Moves with the MAC

He that will not apply new remedies must expect new evils; for time is the greatest innovator.

A. J. BALFOUR
"OF INNOVATIONS"

The 10/8 moving average channel (MAC) is one of my favorite methods for trading in stocks. This timing and trend tool is highly versatile and can be used in all time frames, provided trading volume is sufficient. While this method is by no means fail-safe or foolproof, it does seem to have considerable validity in spotting trend changes and in providing specific support and resistance levels for buying and selling within an existing market trend.

Based on my analyses and observations, I believe that the MAC may be more reliable in stocks than it is in futures. Here is a simple explanation of the methodology and its applications, along with three current examples.

- Calculate two moving averages daily. *MA1 is a 10-period simple MA of the highs, while MA2 is an 8-period simple MA of the lows.*
- A change in trend from *down* to *up* is signaled upon two consecutive periods whose price range is completely *above* the 10-period MA of highs. *This triggers a buy signal.*
- A change in trend from *up* to *down* is signaled upon two consecutive periods whose price range is completely *below* the 8-period MA of lows. *This triggers a sell signal.*

- Once a *buy* signal is in effect, the 8-period MA of lows serves as support.
- Once a *sell* signal is in effect, the 10-period MA of highs serves as resistance.

Figures 10-1 through 10-3 illustrate this condition in Yahoo!, Compaq, and UAL Corp. Note the following analyses.

Yahoo! Inc.:   The trend turned bullish at point B (see Figure 10-1), following a sell at point A. From point B to point C there were *no sell signals*. In fact, the arrows show points where prices touched or fell below the 8 MA of lows. In other words, these were all support levels at which a long position could have been taken. Point C was a sell signal.

COMPAQ Computer Corp.:   The trend turned bullish (see Figure 10-2) at point A. Subsequent to the buy signal at point A, there were *no sell signals* until point B. In fact, there were 12 tests of support, and all but one was a buying opportunity according to my 10/8 MA rules. At point B there was a sell signal, which was reversed to a buy at point C. Support was tested successfully at points D and E.

Figure 10-1. 10/8 MAC on a daily chart of Yahoo! Inc.

Figure 10-2. 10/8 MAC on a daily Compaq Computer Corp. chart.

Figure 10-3. 10/8 MAC on a daily chart of UAL Corp.

While the MAC is not the ultimate system, it does provide valuable information on the current trend, trend change, and support/resistance within established trends. If you're looking to trade ultra-short-term moves, you can use the 10/8 on an intraday basis with 60-minute or 30-minute charts.

In more volatile stocks you can use time frames as small as 10 minutes, although this is recommended only for the most aggressive traders. Another aspect of the MAC is that its buy and sell signals can be confirmed with another timing indicator such as momentum or momentum divergence.

UAL Corp.:   Finally, as a point of information, consider the daily MAC chart of UAL (Figure 10-3). Note that from the last daily sell signal in January 2000, there were four tests of resistance, followed by a buy signal and new uptrend at point B.

The Intraday MAC Method

The 10/8 MAC can also be used on an intraday basis using 5-, 10-, and 30-minute time frames. Figure 10-4 shows the following: At point B, the MAC

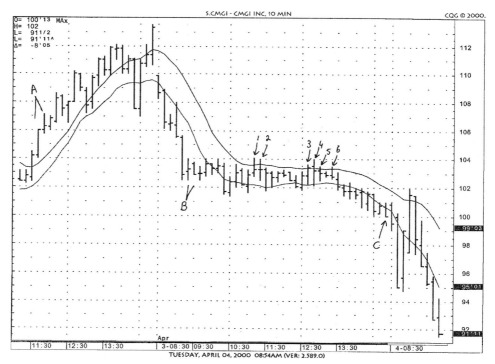

Figure 10-4. MAC signals on a 10-minute CMGI Inc. chart.

gave a sell signal after first giving a buy signal at point A. A short position would have been taken at approximately 103. Exit would have been at point C at the end of the day at about 100. Points 1 through 6 show selling opportunities at resistance.

Capturing the Small Moves with Surgical Timing

The MAC, used on an intraday basis, will assist you in grabbing small moves in the daily time frame. Note that you must be out by the end of the day and that you must wait for a new signal or for resistance from a previous signal on which to establish positions.

Figure 10-5 shows this procedure on a 10-minute chart of eBay and Figure 10-6 also shows this on a 5-minute PMC Sierra Inc. chart. Also note the MAC signals on Figure 10-7, a 10-minute Digital Island chart.

Figure 10-5. MAC on a 10-minute chart of eBay Inc.

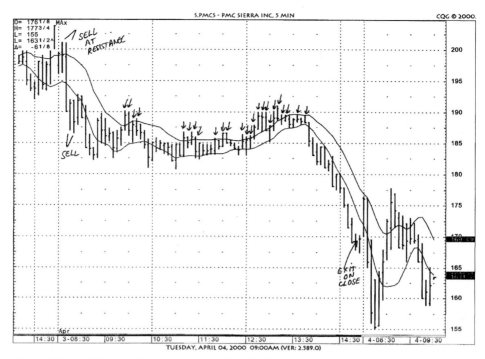

Figure 10-6. MAC on a 5-minute chart of PMC Sierra Inc.

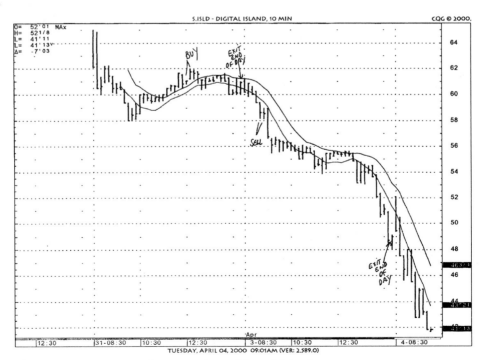

Figure 10-7. MAC on a 10-minute chart of Digital Island.

MAC Application and Rules

Here are the rules of application for the MAC:

- Use the 10-MA of highs/8-MA of lows.
- Buy two consecutive bars above MA of highs.
- Sell two consecutive bars below MA of lows.
- If the trend is *up*, buy at support (MAL).
- If the trend is *down*, sell at resistance (MAH).
- You can use a different time frame for exit.
- You can use options for short-term swings.
- For day traders, enter on the first signal of the day or at support/resistance. Exit on close.

Summary

The MAC has considerable potential for application to intraday trading in stocks. It is, in my experience, one of the most specific and versatile methods. Note that it is a method, as opposed to a system. If you work with it and learn how to apply it, then I believe you can do extremely well in the long run if you are consistent.

11
Day Trading with the MACD

. . . things which would strike us as the ordinary natural way of looking at the universe . . . defeated the greatest intellects for centuries.

IMMANUEL VELIKOVSKY

The moving average convergence/divergence (MACD) was introduced briefly in Chapter 4. This chapter expands on the MACD and its applications, interpretations, assets, and liabilities.

The MACD consists of two indicators. The first is an oscillator, and the second is a moving average of the oscillator. The oscillator is calculated by computing two exponential moving averages and subtracting them. An exponential moving average of the oscillator is then calculated. The result yields two values. Gerald Appel, of Signalert,* has done considerable work with what he calls the MACD (I call it DEMA, or "dual exponential moving average"), particularly in the area of stock index futures. MACD stands for "moving average convergence/divergence." DEMA, as I use it, can be applied to intraday, daily, weekly, and monthly charts.

The basics of the MACD are simple:

- The MACD is a reversing indicator; when a long is closed out, a short is established, and vice versa, if you plan to use MACD as a system.
- Signals are generated when the two MACD values cross.

*Signalert Corporation, 150 Great Neck Road, Great Neck, NY 11021.

Figure 11-1 is a chart of the MACD without price. I have marked the buy and sell signals accordingly. Figure 11-2 is the same MACD plot with price above it and with buy/sell signals. I suggest you examine the MACD as a potentially valuable tool for day trading.

Calculations and Formulae

The MACD can be calculated according to the following formulae and procedures:

1. Determine the length of the exponential moving average. The first step is calculating the coefficient using this formula:

$$\text{Coefficient} = \frac{2}{n+1}$$

where n = number of time units in the moving average. (For the sake of example, we'll choose nine periods.)

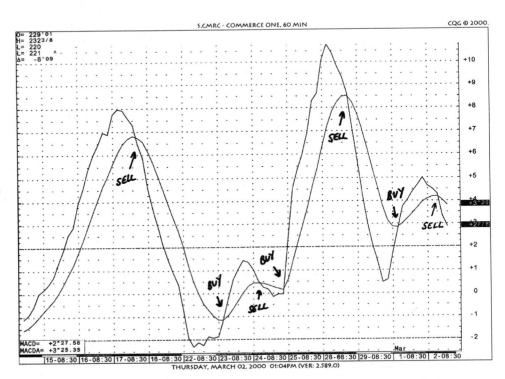

Figure 11-1. Ideal MACD oscillator signals on a 60-minute Commerce One chart.

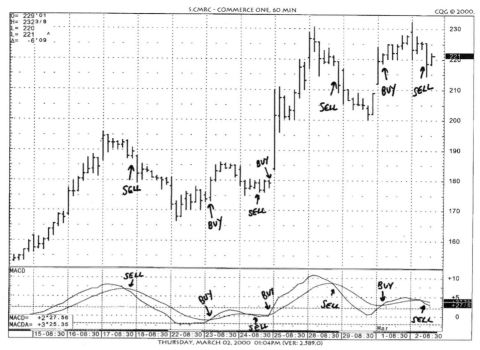

Figure 11-2. MACD buy and sell signals on a 60-minute Commerce One chart.

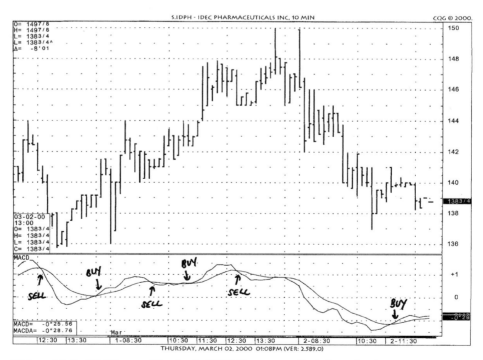

Figure 11-3. MACD on a 10-minute IDEC Pharmaceuticals Inc. chart.

2. Compute the MA as follows:
   Value = (closing price − MA × coefficient) + previous value
3. Compute the second exponential average, using the same procedure.
4. Subtract one from the other. This gives you the *oscillator* value.
5. Calculate an exponential MA of the oscillator. This gives you the *average* value.

The oscillator and average values are compared with each other for the purpose of generating buy and sell signals. As demonstrated, anyone with a bit of mathematics background can easily calculate these values.

Those who have a Commodity Quote Graphics (CQG) system can input these values and obtain the readings. The intricate mathematical computations of the MACD are worth the "clean" signals it tends to generate. The MACD tends to turn quickly at tops and bottoms. It frequently avoids whipsaw-type signals that could bump you out of the market before a trend has changed direction. Furthermore, the MACD does not become overbought or oversold. It can yield buy or sell signals at virtually any level.

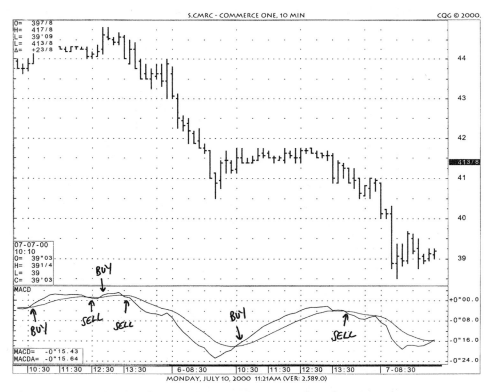

Figure 11-4. MACD signals on a 10-minute Commerce One chart.

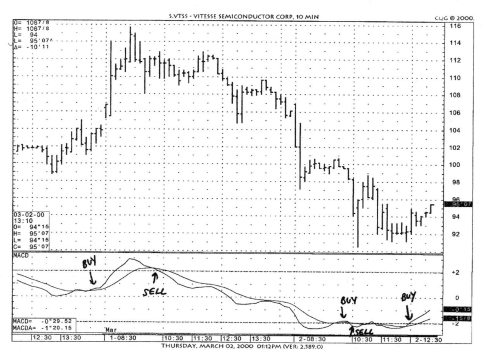

Figure 11-5. Ten-minute MACD signals on a 10-minute chart of Vitesse Semiconductor Corp.

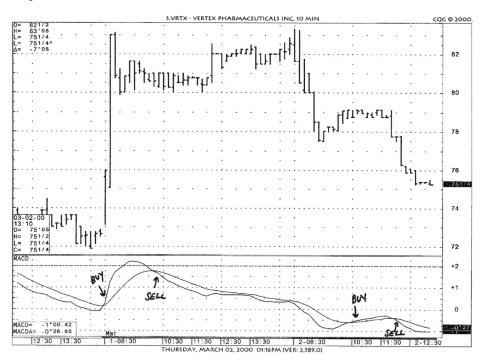

Figure 11-6. Ten-minute MACD signals on a 10-minute chart of Vertex Pharmaceuticals Inc.

The MACD does not require the use of a chart for spotting signals; you need only look at the numbers to see when the values cross. Figures 11-3 through 11-6 are intraday MACD charts. (Note that many contemporary computer analysis and quotation systems have the facilities to generate exponential MAs, so don't let the mathematics dissuade you. You may use simple MAs as opposed to exponential.)

Using the MACD

The precise values used are critical to the sensitivity of the MACD. I use the following values on my Quote Graphics system: 0.213 exponential MA, 0.108 exponential MA, and a 0.199 exponential MA of the difference of the first two MAs. The result is a two-line indicator that generates buy and sell signals on closing crossovers. The MACD, like all timing indicators, is not perfect.

When a market has made a sharp move, up or down, the oscillator values tend to signal a turn in the opposite direction while the market fails to respond as expected. This, of course, is where money management and risk limitation come into play.

Summary

The moving average convergence/divergence (MACD) is a sensitive indicator, originally developed for stock trading on a long-term basis. The day trader can benefit from applying MACD signals on an intraday basis, as illustrated in this chapter. Rather than use the traditional MACD values, I recommend using those listed earlier in this book.

12

Developing Your Own System(s)

*My purpose is to employ facts as tentative
probes, as means of insight or pattern
recognition . . . I want to map new terrain
rather than chart old landmarks . . .*
           MARSHALL McLUHAN

I have emphasized the importance of systematic trading as a prerequisite to
success as a stock day trader. In order to facilitate profitable trading, it is
imperative that you consistently follow an organized trading plan that's as
systematic as possible. In this respect you have several choices. You can buy
a system that has been developed by someone else, you can guess at a system, or you can develop one on your own. Regardless of which approach
you follow, there are a number of things you must know before you take the
plunge into systematic day trading.

The first rule in determining whether to buy or develop your own trading system is to determine your goals as a trader. By this I mean things such
as risk, volatility, drawdown, and stop-loss size. Unless this type of information is available in an off-the-shelf system, you will be better off developing one on your own.

Personally, I feel that you are better off developing your own system than
you are buying one from a system vendor. In most cases, trading systems
that are sold to the public have be beautified to make them more attractive
to the buyer. This means more money for the system seller, more hope for

the system buyer, and less likelihood of profitable results as well as more wasted time for the system buyer.

A trading system provides the following features:

- It contains purely objective rules for market entry and exit.
- It contains risk management rules such as stop loss and trailing stop loss.
- It tells you which markets to trade and when to trade them.
- It can be back-tested using the indicated rules in order to test its validity.
- Its signals are not subject to interpretation—they are operational and repeatable.
- Historical back-test performance provides key statistics and hypothetical results.
- Different traders should be able to get exactly the same signals using similar inputs.

There are other fine details that characterize a trading system; however, the ones indicated here are the most salient. Although these features can be implemented specifically and without interpretation, some people are unable to follow a trading system due to their lack of discipline. They would much rather wallow in subjective indicators than have the self-confidence and self-discipline to trade a mechanical system.

A Rational Approach to System Development

I do not oppose optimizing trading systems; however, I do favor a rational approach to this procedure. My rule of thumb is simple: your trading system should have no more than four to six variables, as well as a reasonable combination of stop-loss and trailing stop-loss amounts. But this is where the optimization should end.

The more variables you build into the system, the less likely will be the future performance of the parameters. Another aspect of system development relates to market personality—a topic that has received little attention by most traders and market analysts. Rather than heavily optimizing a system, I recommend tailoring your system to the personality characteristics of the individual markets, provided that such characteristics exist and that they are sufficiently stable.

How to Develop Your Own Stock Day-Trading Systems Using State-of-the-Art Software

With today's state-of-the-art computer software and hardware, the stock day trader can, with relative ease, develop his or her own systems. Although there are only a few major software programs available for developing your own trading system, most of them are reasonably priced and highly sophisticated.

In order to develop your own stock day-trading systems you will need to have a certain amount of equipment, some good ideas about the systems you want to develop, and some skill at programming the ideas. Don't let the word *programming* scare you. The system development software programs that are currently available do not require heavy programming skills. They have their own programming languages and some even have built-in system development tools that do not require any knowledge of programming.

What follows is a discussion of what you'll need in order to develop your own day-trading system for stocks.

Software and Hardware Requirements for Creating Effective and Profitable Systems Software

There are several popular programs on the market that will allow you to develop and back-test your trading systems. Inasmuch as progress in this area is rapid, the odds are that by the time you read this book there will be even more programs and more functional changes to the existing programs. As a general guideline, however, I suggest that you look for the following features in a system development program:

- The ability to write your own systems using built-in features of the program or the ability to develop your own system using built-in trading system modules
- Real-time live data tracking for systems, methods, and indicators programmed via the system
- The availability of detailed historical performance summaries on the systems you develop
- System signal reports when new timing signals develop
- The ability to program in trailing stop losses

- Audible and/or visual alerts when timing signals occur
- The ability to use position dollar risk management rules with your systems
- The ability to track numerous markets at the same time
- Multiple screens either on the same monitor or on several monitors
- The ability to connect to the Internet or via modem for electronic order placement
- The ability to add codes for systems, methods, or indicators developed by a third party

With these features you should be able to develop and back-test your system ideas effectively, arriving at a realistic picture of how they may have performed in the past as well as a "walk forward" tracking of how they are doing at the present time. By allowing you to generate timing signals in real time, your software will make the task of day trading that much easier as well as more potentially profitable.

Hardware.   Clearly, the better your computer hardware, the faster your system testing will run and the more data you'll be able to store and analyze. A large hard drive is a necessity, as are fast processing speed and considerable memory. It would also be a good idea to have a read/write CD (CD-RW) drive on which to store your data and back up your systems. Given the rapid and continuing advances in computer hardware, I suggest that your best alternative is to use a state-of-the-art system that conforms to the general requirements noted here.

Historical Data.   In order to effectively back-test a day-trading system (or any other system for that matter), you will need a fairly lengthy tick-by-tick data history. This data is available from many vendors at a reasonable price; however, price should not be your major consideration. Here are the factors to evaluate when buying a historical database:

- Is the data accurate and correct?
- Does the data adjust for stock splits?
- Is the data in the correct format required by the system-testing software you are using?
- Can the data be appended in real time once you have finished your system testing and development?
- Are all stocks covered or are only selected stocks covered in the data history?

- Do you really need tick-by-tick data on all stocks or only on higher-volume stocks?
- Does the data vendor provide ongoing and effective technical support?

Make your data purchasing decisions within these parameters.

The Do's and Don'ts of Day-Trading System Development

In order to develop trading systems that will go forward effectively in real time, it is important to follow realistic guidelines. The versatile system development software that is available to today's traders can be used to produce systems long on sex appeal but impotent in real-time application.

The perennial issue for the trader is to avoid overoptimization of trading systems. In short, *just because a system looks good on paper does not mean it will perform well in real time.*

The essence of issues related to this important problem is discussed in a later section in this chapter, entitled "Optimization: The Assets and Liabilities." Generally, the following guidelines should be followed when developing trading systems:

Do's

- *Do* begin with a valid market-timing indicator.
- *Do* build into the system risk management as well as a trailing stop.
- *Do* use a time frame within which you can realistically trade.
- *Do* back-test stocks that have had a history of sufficient liquidity.
- *Do* back-test at least three years of prices.

Don'ts

- *Don't* overly optimize your systems.
- *Don't* back-test your system with stocks that are too volatile for you to trade.
- *Don't* use initial stop losses and trailing stop losses that are too small.

Categories of Systems

There are numerous different trading systems, a number of which are ideally structured for use in stocks.

Trend-Following Systems: What They Are and How They Work

Trend-following systems attempt to do what their name implies. They seek out the start of a new trend and they follow that trend until they are either stopped out or the trend changes. While such systems seek to fulfill a lofty goal, many fail in their efforts. The reason for their failure is simply that the logic of most trend-following systems is not valid.

Trend-following systems have difficulty in determining when a trend has really changed or when the apparent change in trend is merely a temporary fluctuation. Hence, such systems tend to be low in accuracy due to the many false starts. Trend-following systems can do extremely well when they can get you aboard a trend when it begins. But the problem with many such systems is that they cannot reliably grab onto a new trend. I believe that this is because many traders do not have the necessary tools to evaluate a trend correctly or, for that matter, to spot a new trend reliably early on.

Another problem with trend-following systems is that once they have gotten hold of a trend, they tend to wait too long to exit or reverse when the trend has changed. I will give you some suggestions for improving the performance of your trend-following systems, and I will give you some examples of trend-following systems that can be used in stock day trading. Note that I am not opposed to the use of such systems. However, I do believe that many traders cannot use such systems effectively since they do not incorporate effective and appropriate risk management procedures.

Moving-Average-Based Systems

The vast majority of trend-following systems are based on moving averages or a combination of various moving averages. These systems are notoriously poor in their accuracy and timing since they are essentially lagging systems. In other words, they lag behind the market.

As an example, consider the System Report shown in Figure 12-1. This is typical of most moving-average-based trend-following systems. As you can see from the Performance Summary, the system shows an accuracy of 29 percent over 266 trades. The string of 17 consecutive losing trades makes this system unpalatable and very risky. The average trader would not have been able to trade such a system since the 17 consecutive losing trades would have severely tested his or her patience, not to mention account balances.

The system shows a $500 loss as the average trade ("Avg. trade win & loss"). As you will see from the systems I will present later, we can do much

```
              MovAvg Crossover Exp  S&P 500 Index
              CME-Daily   07/16/1982 - 10/31/1997
                   Performance Summary:  All Trades
Total net profit        $-133750.00    Open position P/L         $12325.00
Gross profit            $524125.00     Gross loss               $-657875.00

Total # of trades              266     Percent profitable              29%
Number winning trades           77     Number losing trades           189

Largest winning trade    $62975.00     Largest losing trade     $-16225.00
Average winning trade     $6806.82     Average losing trade      $-3480.82
Ratio avg win/avg loss        1.96     Avg trade (win & loss)     $-502.82

Max consec. winners              4     Max consec. losers              17
Avg # bars in winners           27     vg # bars in losers              9

Max intraday drawdown   $-206025.00
Profit factor                 0.80     Max # contracts held             1
Account size required   $206025.00     Return on account             -65%

                   Performance Summary:  Long Trades
Total net profit        $140300.00     Open position P/L             $0.00
Gross profit            $414000.00     Gross loss               $-273700.00

Total # of trades              133     Percent profitable              38%
Number winning trades           51     Number losing trades            82

Largest winning trade    $62975.00     Largest losing trade     $-13925.00
Average winning trade     $8117.65     Average losing trade      $-3337.80
Ratio avg win/avg loss        2.43     Avg trade (win & loss)     $1054.89

Max consec. winners              4     Max consec. losers               8
Avg # bars in winners           32     Avg # bars in losers             9

Max intraday drawdown    $-47500.00
Profit factor                 1.51     Max # contracts held             1
Account size required    $47500.00     Return on account             295%

                   Performance Summary:  Short Trades
Total net profit        $-274050.00    Open position P/L         $12325.00
Gross profit            $110125.00     Gross loss               $-384175.00

Total # of trades              133     Percent profitable              20%
Number winning trades           26     Number losing trades           107

Largest winning trade    $32750.00     Largest losing trade     $-16225.00
Average winning trade     $4235.58     Average losing trade      $-3590.42
Ratio avg win/avg loss        1.18     Avg trade (win & loss)    $-2060.53

Max consec. winners              3     Max consec. losers              22
Avg # bars in winners           19     Avg # bars in losers             9

Max intraday drawdown   $-289975.00
Profit factor                 0.29     Max # contracts held             1
Account size required   $289975.00     Return on account             -95%
```

Figure 12-1. Performance summary of dual moving average trend-following system in S&P 500 futures, 1982–1997.

better. The system shown in Figure 12-1 was created with minimal optimization. By using a more optimized approach, we can create a profitable system; however, its ability to remain profitable in the future is questionable.

Parabolic Method

The parabolic method is a trend-following method developed by veteran trader Welles Wilder. The parabolic method tracks the market exponentially. It is highly sensitive to reversals in price that occur subsequent to a period of strong acceleration up or down. The parabolic method provides a specific price for each time unit (i.e., daily, weekly, monthly, and hourly), which, if penetrated, most likely signals a change in trend. You can use the parabolic indicator as a stop-loss method.

As long as the market is rising at a steady rate, it will remain above its trigger number generated by the parabolic method. Once this number has been penetrated on the downside, the trend is considered down. The reverse holds true for markets that are in downtrends. In other words, when a trend is down, there will be a parabolic buy-stop number above the market. In this case a change in trend occurs when the parabolic buy stop has been penetrated.

The parabolic is an excellent method, provided it can be harnessed into a system using risk management and an effective trailing stop-loss procedure. A day trading system that uses the parabolic indicator as its timing method can be very effective in stocks.

There are many other trend-following indicators, systems, and methods. While trend-following systems have their distinct limitations, I believe that you can overcome many of these by the judicious use of indicators, timing methods, and risk management.

Breakout Systems: What They Are and How They Work

A breakout system attempts to overcome the limitations of trend-following systems by trading only when the market surpasses a predetermined resistance point (buy breakout) or falls below a predetermined support point (sell breakout). These systems tend to be considerably more accurate than do trend-following systems, and they tend to produce larger average profits.

Strengths and Weaknesses of Breakout Systems. Breakout systems are subject to the limitations inherent in trend-following systems. They can be victims of false breakouts. If the logic used in defining a breakout for the purpose of generating a signal is faulty, then there will be numerous false signals. Notwithstanding these limitations, breakout systems are particularly effective in today's volatile markets, such as Treasury bonds, currencies, and stock index futures.

Range Breakout Systems. Such systems focus on buying (and/or reversing positions) when prices penetrate certain levels of resistance and selling short (and/or reversing positions) when prices penetrate certain levels of support. Inherent in this idea is the belief that markets move through levels of resistance and support and that once these levels have been penetrated, fairly strong moves in the direction of the penetration can be expected.

The belief is likely a correct one, based not only on observational experience but also on valid systems that have been developed on the basis of this concept. The most well-known breakout systems were developed by Chester Keltner. Also noteworthy in the original work on this type of system is Nicholas Darvas, who expounded on the box theory of price movement in stocks. The concept of such systems is simple. Once prices have made a new high for a given period of time or a new low for a given period of time, buy or sell signals are triggered accordingly.

Range Relationships

During every trading day or time frame (month, week, year, hour, minute, etc.) there are four prices that describe or summarize the price activity. Each time segment yields an *opening*, a *closing*, a *high*, and a *low* price. These prices are very important inasmuch as they tell us who is in control of the market. By *control,* I do not mean control in the sense of manipulation, but rather in the sense of who has the upper hand in terms of the trend. In addition to this, the range or average price of the day is important.

When the bulls are in control of a market, prices tend to close near the high of their day, more often than they tend to close near their low of the day. When the bears are in control, prices tend to close near their low of the day more often than they close near their high of the day.

While the relationship between the closing price and the opening price is very important, the relationship between the ranges over several days is important. Markets that are in bull trends as well as markets that are about to enter new bull trends tend to show a specific range relationship. Range breakout systems attempt to take advantage of these relationships, producing buy and sell signals depending upon the exact configuration range and its derivatives.

Market Pattern Systems: What They Are and How They Work

Trading systems based on market patterns have received insufficient attention over the years because back-testing was laborious and frequently insufficient due to the difficulty in writing objective algorithms and the limited computer power available to test such systems. Virtually unlimited computer power can now be applied to thorough system tests over millions of combinations and iterations to adequately quantify the performance characteristics of pattern-based systems.

As an example of a pattern-based system, consider the following algorithm:

> **If Tuesday's high is greater than Monday's open and last Friday's high, then buy on a ½-point penetration of Monday's high on Tuesday. Use a $3 stop loss below the lowest low of the last 10 trading sessions and exit on the _n_th profitable opening.**

This is an example of a fairly elementary market pattern that can be quickly tested via computer but which was exceedingly difficult to validate or even back-test prior to the development of today's advanced computer systems.

Among today's most effective market pattern systems, we find methods that compare multiple day open, high, close, and low relationships with timing indictors and a variety of trend filters.

Strengths and Weaknesses of Market Pattern Systems. The good news about pattern-based systems is that they frequently anticipate market moves, as opposed to lagging indicators such as moving indicators, which usually follow market moves.

Furthermore, pattern-based indicators tend to reveal subtle changes in the underlying indication and distribution of contracts and/or shares by market professionals, large traders, managed funds, and insiders. The bad news about market pattern systems is that there are literally thousands of combinations that must be tested. The trader could easily spend a lifetime researching different patterns and combinations of patterns.

Support and Resistance Systems: What They Are and How They Work

Systems that are based on support and resistance depend on an active determination of the underlying trend and then take action depending upon the trend. In a market that is trending higher these systems will buy when prices decline to predetermined support levels, while in a declining market they will sell short at predetermined resistance levels.

The success of these systems is a direct function of how accurate the determination of trend, support, and resistance has been. The vast majority of methods available today for making such determinations are either inaccurate, based on myth as opposed to fact, or otherwise specious.

Strengths and Weaknesses of Support and Resistance Systems. Clearly, the limitation of such systems is their ability, or lack thereof, to accurately determine the three major variables necessary for success. Furthermore, such methods frequently fail to capture major market moves, but rather focus their attention on short-term swings.

Arguably, such an approach can be criticized for failing to fulfill the dictum that "the big money is made in the big move." By focusing on the smaller moves, the trader may miss the bigger move. I believe, however, that it is possible to capture both moves with a good degree of accuracy.

Artificial Intelligence (AI) Systems: How They Work

Although an entire book (or for that matter, several books) could be written on the subject of artificial intelligence, I will make this coverage brief and to the point. The essence of artificial intelligence–based systems is that they attempt to combine a multiplicity of indicators, inputs, systems, and methods in order to arrive at the best combination.

Then, by analyzing previous losses, these systems supposedly "learn" from and "correct" their mistakes. In the future, artificial intelligence systems will become increasingly complex and may even prove successful in generating profits. Today, I am unimpressed with such methods, with the exception of a few that seem to hold promise as the systems of tomorrow.

The elements of contemporary artificial intelligence systems are as follows:

- A learning model that comprises the "brain" of the neural net (NN)
- Layers of analysis in which the variables are weighted as to their effect on the overall learning
- A learning mode in which the system is "trained"
- A forward mode during which the neural system goes ahead trading on its own with the base of knowledge that it has accumulated during its training period

Strengths and Weaknesses of Artificial Intelligence Systems. It has been said that current artificial intelligence systems are nothing more than sophisticated optimization programs that curve-fit the past market behavior perfectly, but which do not perform up to expectations. The reality of such systems is that they are still in their infancy and cannot yet be fully judged as to their future performance.

More time is needed to develop and evaluate neural nets. I believe that as we learn more about the variables and components that constitute market behavior, we will also learn more about developing effective and profitable AI and NN systems for trading.

Why Test Trading Systems?

Traders test systems for various reasons. Some test a system merely to say they've done so, only to disregard the outcome or to accept mediocre results, rationalizing the negative aspects of the system. Other traders test systems in order to sell them to the public—their goal is to optimize systems in order to show maximum performance. Then there's the serious trader who tests systems to achieve several goals, including but not limited to the following:

- *To determine whether a theory or hypothetical construct is valid* in historical testing
- *To summarize the overall hypothetical performance of a system* and to analyze its various aspects in order to isolate its strong and weak points
- *To determine how different timing indicators interact* with one another to produce an effective trading system
- *To explore the interaction of risk and reward variables* (stop loss, trailing stop loss, position size, etc.) that would have returned the best overall performance with the smallest drawdown

Test Your Trading System

While it may seem that the last item in the preceding list refers to optimization, you will see from the discussion of optimization later that it is not optimization according to my definition of the term. The purpose of testing systems is simply to find what will work best for you based on what appears to have worked in the past. In so doing, *we must remember that what worked in hypothetical testing may not necessarily work in the future.* A thorough test of your trading system should include at least the following information.

Number of Years Analyzed.   Although it is desirable to test as much data as possible, many trading systems and indicators do not withstand the test of time. The further back you test, the less effective most systems will be. Many system developers test only 10 years of historical data since that best shows their systems. You must make your own decision regarding the length of your test.

Number of Trades Analyzed.   More important than the number of years analyzed is the number of trades. You need not analyze many years of data if you have a large sample size of trades. I recommend at least 100 trades, providing your system will generate this number of trades in back-testing.

If you are truly interested in determining the effectiveness of your system, the more trades you test, the better.

Remember that there will always be a tendency to test fewer trades when you realize that the system is not holding up under back-testing. Some traders argue that the factors underlying market trends 25 years ago were distinctly different from those during the past 10 years. They feel that testing 25 years of data distorts the picture. If they are correct, how would we know when the current market forces change and that we must, therefore, change our trading systems? We are much better off finding systems that work in all types of markets.

Maximum Drawdown.   This is one of the most important aspects of a trading system. A very large drawdown is a negative factor since it eliminates most traders from the game well before the system would have turned in its positive performance. Since most traders are not well capitalized, they cannot withstand a large drawdown. However, drawdown is a function of account size. Obviously a $15,000 drawdown in a $100,000 account is not unusual; however, the same drawdown in a $25,000 account is serious. You may decide to risk large drawdown in order to achieve outstanding performance, but this is your decision.

Consider also the source of the drawdown by examining the largest losing trade. If the majority of the drawdown occurred on only one trade, you will be better off than if the *drawdown was spread out over numerous successive losses.*

Maximum Consecutive Losses.   This performance variable is more psychological than anything else is. An otherwise excellent trading system may have lost money on many trades in succession. Few traders can maintain their discipline through four or more successive losing trades. Even after the third loss, many find ways of changing it.

However, at times it is necessary to weather the storm of 10 or more successive losses. If you know ahead of time what the worst-case scenario has been, you will be prepared. That's why it's important for your system test to give you this information.

Largest Single Losing Trade.   This important piece of information indicates how much the maximum drawdown is the result of a single losing trade. And this allows you to adjust the initial stop loss in retesting the system so as to see how large the average losing trade has been. If the average losing trade was, for example, $1055 and the largest single loser was $8466, you can readily see that a good portion of the average losing trade was a function of the largest loser. This shows that if you had had a better way of managing the large loser (in hindsight, of course), your overall system performance would have been considerably better.

I strongly recommend close examination of the trade that resulted in the single largest loss if this loss is clearly much higher than the average losing trade. Another question to ask is this: Why was the largest single losing trade so much larger than the stop loss selected? A single largest losing trade that is several times larger than your selected stop loss points to a potential problem, perhaps with the system test. You must investigate further in such cases.

Largest Single Winning Trade.   Perhaps more important than the largest single losing trade is the largest single winning trade. If, for example, your hypothetical profits total $96,780, and $33,810 of this is attributed to only one trade, you have a distorted average trade figure. It's often a good idea to remove this one trade from the overall results and recomputerize them in order to show the performance without this extraordinary winner.

You may find that the system you have tested is mediocre, perhaps even a loser, when the single largest trade has been eliminated from the performance summary. If you can wait 10 years for one big trade, then use the system—but do it against my advice. *What you're looking for in any system with regard to average winning and losing trades is consistency—far more important than one or two extremely large winning trades that give a distorted performance picture.*

On this occasion, only two trades may account for a considerable portion of the net system profits. While some traders feel that this somehow diminishes the value of the system, I disagree. As long as at least one-half of the overall system performance is due to trades other than the largest single winning long and short trade combined, the system is valid. As far as numbers are concerned, I would not use any system that, after deducting reasonable slippage and commission as well as the largest single long and short winners, does not show at least $100 average profit per trade.

More important, because a large portion of profits in many systems derives from a very small number of trades, it is imperative that in each and every trade you adhere as closely to the rules as possible. Trading systems are not money machines; they don't grind out one profit after another. Trading systems make their money on the bottom line. There are many losers and few winners.

The losers are kept in check by using money management stop losses that must, in most cases, be reasonably large. And the winners, only a few of which are very large, make the game worth the candle. The trader who can't stick with a position, or let it ride, is the trader who will be sorely disappointed with the results because the big winners will be cut short.

Winning Trades. This statistic is not nearly as important as one might think. In actuality, few systems have more than 65 percent winning trades and the more trades in your sample, the smaller this figure will be. Systems that are correct as little as 30 percent of the time can still be good systems and systems that are accurate as much as 80 percent of the time can be bad systems. It's easy to see that even a high degree of accuracy with a large average losing trade and a small average winning trade does not make a good system.

Average Trade. This statistic will tell you what the average hypothetical trade has been. You must make certain that when you test your system you deduct slippage and commission from your average trade. Commissions add up—even discount commissions. And slippage is an important factor when determining system performance.

As a rule of thumb, I recommend deducting between $75 and $100 per trade for slippage and commission. Once this has been done, you will often significantly reduce the average trade figure. As I pointed out earlier, you must also pay close attention to the largest winning trade and the largest losing trade when evaluating the average trade. The average trade figure is important since it considers all profits, all losses, slippage, and commission.

Optimization: The Assets and Liabilities

When it comes to trading system optimization, there has been considerable controversy. What exactly is wrong with an optimizing system? Can you go too far? Is there a happy medium? The real issues in system optimization are complex and they've been exacerbated by the tendency of system developers to optimize their programs above and beyond any reasonable degree. To optimize a system is to discover the parameters that provide the best results in hypothetical back-testing. In other words, optimization is a form of discovering what would have produced the best results using numerous if-then scenarios.

Previous to the availability of affordable computer hardware and software, optimization was a long and laborious procedure. In order to discover the best fit, the systems developer would need to repeatedly backtrack and test several variables. If the system parameters were numerous, the process was virtually impossible. Obviously, computers have made this a quick and efficient task. Now any trader with several thousand dollars can develop optimized systems.

Such ease of testing and optimizing is both good and bad. On one hand, it allows traders to develop, test, and refine (i.e., optimize) systems much more rapidly. On the other hand, it has opened the door to what is called *curve fitting*. The simple fact is that the powerful system-testing programs now available allow traders as well as system vendors to repeatedly test a host of timing variables, stop losses, and other risk management schemes in order to determine which combinations would have produced the best results. In effect, this procedure fits the best parameters on past history to produce the best hypothetical results. However, the conclusions reached by such methods are often specious.

The trader who tests and retests to find out the best fit will eventually reach his or her goal, but the goal itself may be nothing more than a reflection of the curve-fitted results. Tests tell us what has worked in the past, but may not reveal anything worthwhile about the future. Since the past is not a carbon copy of the future, it is doubtful that excessively optimized parameters will work in the future.

The more parameters in the decision-making model, the less likely they are to work in the future. Overly optimized results lead to false conclusions. The result will likely mean losses. For those who develop and sell trading systems as a business, optimization is an amazing tool that allows the creation of outstanding hypothetical performance results that in turn allow systems developers to make incredible claims. And claims sell systems.

Summary

This chapter reviewed the issues regarding system development, testing, and optimization. In addition, guidelines were given for hardware and software requirements as well as the do's and don'ts of system development.

13

Momentum Divergence

While I see many hoof-marks going in, I see none coming out.

AESOP

Momentum, used as an indicator, and the momentum moving average, used as a timing signal, have already been discussed in Chapter 9. I believe that momentum is one of the most powerful, yet one of the least understood, indicators available to traders. As you may recall from my previous discussions of momentum, its importance and uses are severalfold. It has the following characteristics:

- Bullish momentum (i.e., momentum becoming more positive) correlates closely with rising prices.
- Bearish momentum (i.e., momentum becoming more negative) correlates closely with declining prices.
- Momentum crossing from negative to positive indicates that a new bull trend is probably beginning.
- Momentum crossing from positive to negative indicates that a new bear trend is probably beginning.
- Momentum rising while price is falling indicates bullish divergence and the possibility of a low.
- Momentum declining while price is rising indicates bearish divergence and the possibility of a top.

As prices rise so should momentum. As prices decline so should momentum. Not all tops and bottoms develop in conjunction with momentum divergence; however, many do. The task of the trader is to find periods of divergence and to use them with timing in order to spot trading opportunities. In order to do so we must first define an operational procedure for finding divergence.

Once we have found the period of divergence we must have an objective method of generating buy and sell signals. And once we have defined an objective method for generating buy and sell signals we will also need a method for following up the trade. Let's begin with basics and move to the details of my methodology.

Spotting Divergence

The key to any method of analysis based on an indicator that may be subject to different interpretations is to define as operational a methodology as possible. In order to do so we must first know how to find periods of bullish or bearish divergence. I use the following rules (note the accompanying examples).

- Look for periods of time during which the 28-period momentum and price move in different directions over a time frame of at least six units. By this I mean that at least six price bars (of whatever length you define) must be included in the divergence period. Figures 13-1 and 13-2 show precisely what I mean by this definition. Figures 13-3 and 13-4 show actual examples of bullish and bearish divergence, respectively.

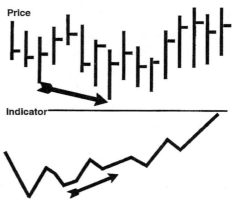

Figure 13-1. Ideal example of bullish divergence. This ideal example shows bullish divergence, since momentum is rising while prices are still declining. The ultimate resolution of this situation should be an upturn in price, since momentum tends to lead price.

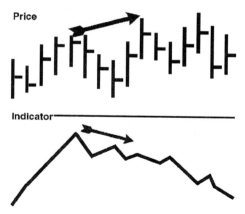

Figure 13-2. Ideal example of bearish divergence on. This ideal example shows bullish divergence, since momentum is declining while prices are still rising. The ultimate resolution of this situation should be a downturn in price, since momentum tends to lead price.

Figure 13-3. Actual example of bullish divergence on a five-minute chart of Digital Island. As price continues to decline (A-B), momentum continues to increase (C-D). The outcome of this situation is an upward surge in prices that occurs after low point B. Previous to point A (which corresponds to momentum point C), a bearish divergence occurred at points 1-2 and 3-4; however, the divergence lasted for only five price bars, therefore failing to meet our minimum requirement. Nevertheless, prices still declined sharply thereafter.

Figure 13-4. Actual example of bearish divergence on a five-minute chart of Nextel Communications Inc. This shows bearish divergence developing at points A-B and C-D. Previous to points A and C, price and momentum tracked one another without any divergence.

- Once you have found the bullish or bearish divergence period you must find the *divergence breakout point* (DBP) for the given divergence period. The DBP will give you timing signals that you will need in order to enter a trade.

- The *buy DBP* (DBP+) is defined as the highest momentum point during the divergence period.

- The *sell DBP* (DBP–) is defined as the lowest momentum point during the divergence period.

Figures 13-5 and 13-6 illustrate the DBP+ and the DBP– as defined once the period of divergence has been found.

- *As soon as the DBP+ has been penetrated on a* closing *basis for the indicated price bar, then* buy *on opening of the next bar.* This will mean that you will use a buy at market order. In other words, as soon as the price bar has ended and the DBP+ is penetrated, you will buy at the market. If you are short, then you will reverse your position to a long.

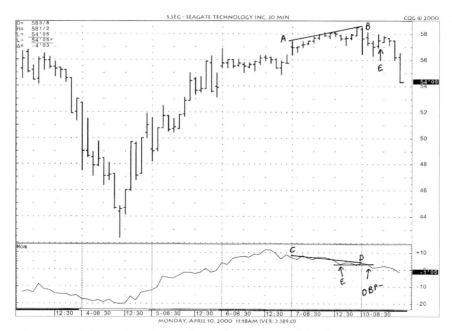

Figure 13-5. DBP–. This figure shows development of the divergence breakout point on the short side. Bearish divergence occurs from A-B and C-D. Point E, the momentum low between C and D, is the breakout point. It is penetrated on the opening of 4/10. Price follows through to the downside.

Figure 13-6. DBP+. This shows bullish divergence from A-B and C-D, and point E penetrated to the upside. This constitutes a buy signal with follow-through on the upside thereafter. A stop loss would have captured a good portion of this move before it turned lower.

- *As soon as the DBP– has been penetrated on a* closing *basis for the indicated price bar, then* sell *on opening of the next bar.* This will mean that you will use a sell at market order. In other words, as soon as the price bar has ended and the DBP– is penetrated, you will sell short at the market. If you are long them, you will reverse your position from long to short.

- *Once you have been filled, either on the long side or the short side, you will exit your trade, either at a specific profit target, at a reversing signal, at a stop loss, or at the end of the day (since this is a day-trading method).*

Figures 13-7 through 13-12 illustrate specific examples of this approach. Please take some time to examine them in order to understand the method better.

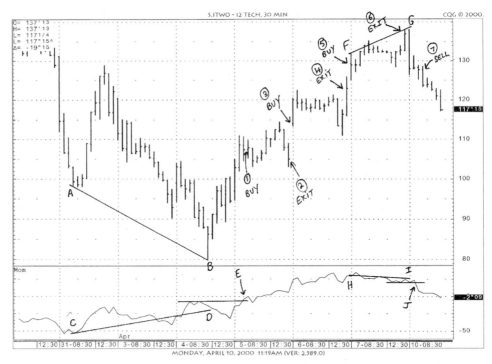

Figure 13-7. Momentum divergence buy and sell signals on a 30-minute chart of 12 Tech. This chart shows bullish divergence at A-B and C-D, a breakout and buy signal at E, and bearish divergence at F-G and H-I, with a sell signal at J. In a day trade, you would have been a buyer at point 1, closing out the trade at end of the day, point 2, at a small loss. The next day the signal from point E is still valid and you would have bought at point 3. You would be out at the end of the day at point 4. The next day signal E is still valid. You would have bought at point 5 and exited at point 6, again at a profit. The next day bearish divergence is clearly developing. You would have gone short at point 7, exiting at a profit at the end of the day.

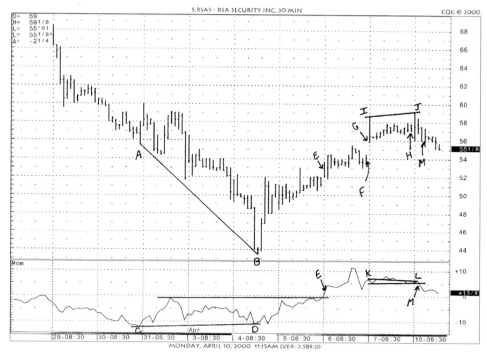

Figure 13-8. Momentum divergence signals on a 30-minute chart of RSA Security Inc. Bullish divergence at A-B and C-D; buy signal at E. Exit at a small profit at F. Buy again the next day on open, G. Exit at a small profit at the end of the day, H. Bearish divergence developing at I-J and K-L. Short position taken at M. Market follows through to the downside. Exit would have been at the end of the day at 51% (not shown on the chart).

Importance of Exiting at the End of the Day

As you know from the preceding discussion, the method as described herein is for the purpose of day trading. Ideally, you can use either the 5-, 10-, 15-, 20-, or 30-minute charts. Each time frame will yield different results. The time frame you use should be a function of the trading volume and volatility of the stock(s) you are day trading. Stocks with heavier volume and more intraday price volatility can be traded using time frames from 5 to 15 minutes, whereas those with less activity and volatility can be traded with longer time-frame price bars, such as 30 minutes.

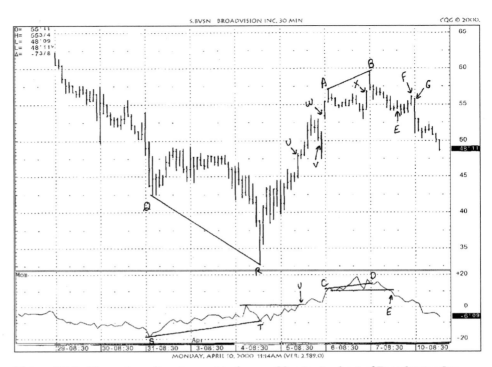

Figure 13-9. Momentum divergence signals on a 30-minute chart of Broadvision Inc. Bullish divergence at QRST results in a buy signal at point U. Long from U closed at a small profit at U. Long again at W and out at a profit at X. Bearish divergence develops at A-B and C-D. Short position taken at E. Closed out at a small loss at F. Short again at G. Profitable as of the end of the chart.

In practice, the 30-minute bar tends to be preferred. In any event, if you enter a trade with the intention of making it a day trade, then you must exit at the end of the day session. On some occasions (in heavily traded stocks), you may want to exit in the after-hours session; however, note that I have not tested this procedure adequately to attest to its efficacy. In other words, you're on your own in such cases. Figures 13-13 and 13-14 illustrate two more examples using 30-minute data.

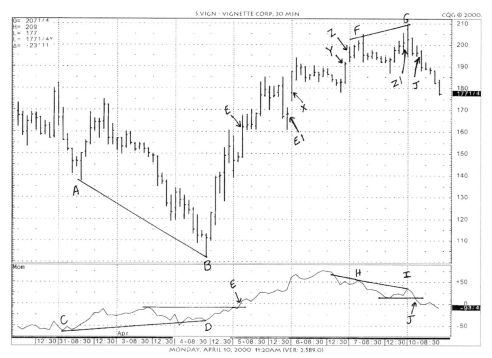

Figure 13-10. Momentum divergence signals on a 30-minute chart of Vignette Corp. Bullish divergence at A-B and C-D; buy signal at E. Closed out at E1. In this case, from the buy point at about 161, a move to 185 would have resulted in sufficient profit for a trailing stop. Therefore, the trade would have been closed out at a profit well before point E1. Buy again the next day at X; out at a profit at Y. Buy the next day at Z. Exit at the end of the day, at Z1, for a small profit. Bearish signal occurs at J and a short position is taken.

Beyond the Day Time Frame

The momentum divergence method as discussed and described here can also be used for trading beyond the day time frame. In such a case it becomes a short-term trading method and you need not exit at the end of the day. You may want to study this approach if you are interested in using it for short-term trading in addition to or instead of day trading.

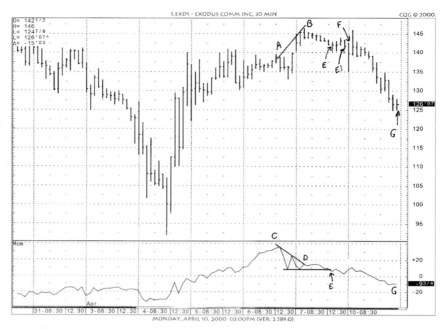

Figure 13-11. Momentum divergence signals on a 30-minute chart of Exodus Communications Inc. Bearish divergence at A-B and C-D. Sell signal at E; closed out at the end of the day at E1. Sell again at F; exit at G.

Figure 13-12. Momentum divergence signals on a 30-minute chart of Medarex, Inc. Bullish divergence at A-B and C-D. Buy signal at E; out at a profit at F. Buy again at G; out at a profit at H. Buy again at I. Stopped out at a loss at J.

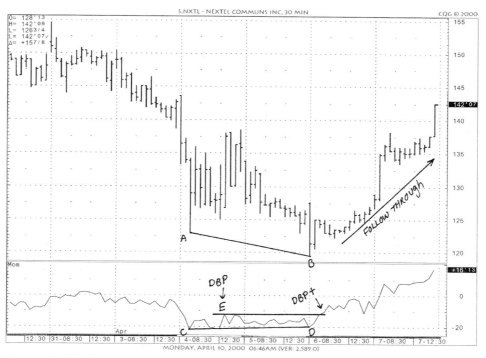

Figure 13-13. Momentum divergence with 30-minute data on a Nextel Communications chart. This chart shows how the momentum divergence method can be used to hold a stock beyond the day time frame. A buy signal occurred at point X, with the penetration of E. This position would still be held as of the end of this chart.

Trading for a Profit Target

You may wish to use this approach with a profit target, in addition to using it with an end-of-day exit. In such cases you could do the following:

- When you enter the trade, take a position of at least 200 shares.
- One hundred shares (or half your position) will be exited at a profit target.
- One hundred shares (or the remaining half of your position) will be closed out at the end of the day.

A profit target can be determined either as a dollar or as a point amount or at a resistance point based on the MAC (see Chapter 4).

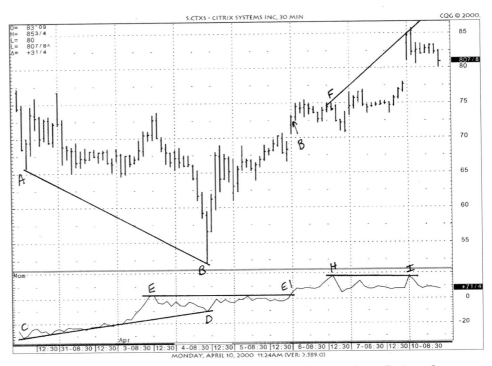

Figure 13-14. Momentum divergence with 30-minute data on a Citrix Systems Inc. chart. This chart illustrates another example of bullish divergence at A-B and C-D, with a buy signal at point E1. The stock would be held, but as bearish divergence develops at F-G and H-I, the stop loss would be raised accordingly to protect the profit.

Stop Loss

As always, it's a good idea to use a stop loss in order to protect your capital. Stop losses should be either at a fixed dollar amount or at a technical point. If your stop is at a fixed dollar amount, then make certain that the stop is not too small. A stop loss that is too conservative (by which I mean too small) will predispose you to getting stopped out most of the time since you have not given the market sufficient room to move within its typical range of prices. A reasonable stop to use would be one that is twice the average daily range of the stock.

Summary

I believe that the momentum divergence method described in this chapter can be very useful in day trading stocks. I have attempted to give you a set of operational and objective rules by which you may apply this approach. If you are interested in this method, then I suggest you spend some time working with it before you attempt to apply it. Since not all stocks will give signals every day, you should maintain charts on a reasonably large number of active stocks, monitoring them daily for the possibility of trading signals.

14

Practical Considerations of Stock Day Trading

The love of money and the love of learning
rarely meet.

GEORGE HERBERT

This chapter will cover a variety of practical but very important considerations. All too often we tend to focus on the goals of trading without sufficient attention to the practical details. Since the weakest link or building block in its structural chain limits the success of any venture, it is important to make certain that your basic elements have been carefully prepared. Although I have attempted to cover all of the important practical aspects of day trading, there may be some situations that I have not addressed.

Here, not necessarily in order of importance, are my views and recommendations regarding the practical aspects of day trading in stocks.

Starting Capital

With the industry and media promotional campaigns that have been so prevalent in recent years, many new and inexperienced traders have been attracted to the markets in the mistaken belief that they can be successful by starting with a relatively small amount of capital. The fact is that the more money you begin with, the greater your odds of success.

Although I am loathe to state a dollar amount, I'd say that if you begin with less than $5000 for day trading stocks, your odds of success will be minimal. To give yourself a good chance, you should consider beginning with at least $25,000. If you do so, then you can trade in several stocks at the same time and in more than 100 shares of each. If you use margin, then you can trade as much as $50,000 worth of stock. You may wish to read my discussion of trading on margin, however, before you decide to do so since trading on margin has its good points as well as its bad points.

Brokerage Account

The more money you can save on commissions, the more money you'll put into your pocket. It is, therefore, in your best interest to keep commissions as low as possible while not sacrificing quality and speed of order execution. If you can get low commissions and fast executions by dealing with a broker that is not online, then do so. Typically, however, online brokers will give you the lowest commissions as well as commission rebates if you trade actively.

In deciding which online brokerage firm to use, consider the following factors:

- How fast can you get access?
- Are free live quotes available?
- Are the quotes quick and accurate?
- Are they streaming quotes?
- Can you get NASDAQ Level II quotes as an active trader?
- Are commission rebates available to active traders?
- Are there backup systems by which you may place an order by telephone if the Internet-based system is inoperative?
- How fast can the brokerage Web site be accessed during heavy traffic times?
- Does the brokerage firm provide you with free access to charts, market statistics, and news (assuming you use these)?
- Can you track your positions and account equity on a real-time basis, tick by tick?
- Is the brokerage firm financially stable?

Computer Hardware and Software

If you decide to use computer-based systems, whether programmed mechanical systems or charts, then please read the details provided in

Chapter 12. Note that you do not need to use a computer to be successful at day trading. In fact, some traders do better without a computer.

Live Quotes

Some traders feel that live quotes are a prerequisite to successful stock day trading. This is not necessarily true. Live quotes can cost a lot of money, and such monies are not necessarily well spent. I have described several methods for day trading that do not require tick-by-tick data. Don't rush into day trading with live data without considerable thought. The cost of live data means that you will have still another expense to overcome on the road to profitable day trading.

Media

Some day traders believe that in order for them to trade successfully they will need to have as much news and information as possible. They read the business newspapers daily. They listen to the business news on radio and television. They subscribe to numerous advisory services. And they search for recommendations and opinions on the Internet.

Typically, the result is more confusion rather than less confusion. And the more confusion there is, the fewer profits there will be in the long run. My advice is to allow only a limited amount of input (if any) from the media. Most traders are unable to cope with the diversity of opinions and news that daily impinges on their discipline. I believe that the best technical trading is done in isolation.

Therefore, I suggest that you isolate yourself from the news. Separate yourself from any and all influences that can weaken your resolve and self-discipline as a day trader. The less information you have about the "news," the better off you will be in the long run. Although you may not believe me now, it will take only a few losses caused by your overreaction to the news to convince you that I am correct.

Time

One good way to lose money is to attempt trading that is too intense or demanding for the amount of time you have on hand. If you don't have the time to watch prices actively during the day, then do not attempt to trade a method that requires you to watch prices every five minutes. Before you make the commitment to trade, determine the time frame within which you will trade and do so on the basis of the time you have available to this venture. Day trading is not a hobby; it's a business. You can't succeed in this business unless you give it the time and attention it deserves.

Risk

Another important consideration is the risk that you want to take each time you trade. Risk and reward are opposite sides of the same coin. Typically, the more risk you take, the greater will be your potential reward. But a larger risk can lead to a large reward only if you have the prerequisite skills to play the game correctly.

The inexperienced trader can take a large risk on a worthless proposition. In such a case inexperience will work against the trader. Yet an experienced trader will know when to take more risk and when to expect more reward for the increased degree of risk. You are better off, as a beginning trader, taking less risk for less potential reward in order to build your account slowly.

What Stocks to Day Trade

Still another concern is how you will determine which stocks to day trade. There are many ways in which to do this. Some of them have been discussed earlier in this book. However, here are a few guidelines that may prove valuable.

- Pick stocks that trade at least 500,000 shares daily.
- Pick stocks that have recently made large moves up and/or down and do your market analyses on these stocks.
- Pick stocks that have a large trading range daily. This is the method I recommend because my trading techniques are most compatible with this approach.
- Trade stocks listed on major exchanges such as the NYSE, the AMEX, or the NASDAQ.
- Try to pick stocks that are favorites of mutual funds. You can determine this by looking at the large stockholders. This information is available online.
- Try to pick stocks that are involved in industries that are currently in favor and that will, as a result, have a large following.

Margin and Margin Calls

Trading on margin involves using money borrowed from your brokerage firm. The broker charges you interest. Although the rate of interest seems small, it can add up over time and it is therefore absurd to trade using margin unless you are able to make more profit than you give up in interest to the broker. Some traders prefer not to trade on margin at all.

If your trades have been going badly and if you are trading on margin, you may overextend your positions and as a result your broker will issue a *margin call* to you. This means that you will either have to add the necessary amount of money to your account, or you will have to sell out stocks from your positions in order to meet the margin call. If you fail to meet the margin call, your broker has the right to liquidate stocks from your account in order to eliminate the call.

Some traders believe that if you get a margin call you have overextended yourself and that you should not meet the call by adding funds to your account. Rather, you should sell out stock to meet the call. A margin call is a warning that your trading is not going well. If you get a margin call, then take heed and reevaluate what you have been doing.

Summary

In order to day trade stocks profitably you will need to have an effective system or method; however, you will also need to consider some practical trading aspects as well. These were covered in this chapter.

15

The Psychology of Day Trading

*Patience and passage of time do more than
strength and fury.*

JEAN DE LA FONTAINE
FABLES

The Dangers of Forecasting

The investing and trading public always has been fascinated with forecasts
and predictions. In my book, *The Handbook of Commodity Cycles* (Wiley,
1982), I discussed the differences between following trends and forcing
trends as they relate to the investor or speculator. Here is what I wrote at
that time:

> It took me about nine years to realize that, although it may be a
> romantic and ego-gratifying goal, forecasting is not necessarily syn-
> onymous with profit. The act of determining where a market is going
> and when it will get there poses for me and for most traders a distinct
> disadvantage in profitable trading because it predisposes one to par-
> ticular expectations.
>
> Expectations are what lead us to misperceive events, misread indica-
> tors, lose confidence in our signals, and avoid implementing decisions
> that we should know will "work."
>
> What should a trader do? I believe that Joseph Granville, legendary
> stock market technician supreme, has one answer. The thing to do is

simply and exclusively to follow the market, because it is the market we are using as the trading vehicle. Granville (1980) says:

"Following Wall Street analysts will seldom make you money but following a good stock market analyst will. We don't buy and sell the economy. We buy and sell stocks. Why do people forever try to link the economy with the stock market?

"Economics have nothing to do with stock market timing—timing is everything. Yet the press will forever clutter up their market commentary with discussions of the economy.

"The first thing to do about the market is get in gear with it. It is never too late to buy stocks as long as the market traffic light is green.

"That remains true even if you are buying stocks one day before a top. Who cares? You would simply follow the market sell signal, sell everything and then go 100% short across the board. That is called following the market."

In short, it is absolutely necessary to follow the market without attempting to impose upon it any preconceived notions. I believe that a market technician can only be a market technician, nothing more, nothing less.

It is not surprising that much of the investment world is preoccupied with the issues of forecasting and predicting. Indeed, I feel that volatile markets and unstable world economies require investors to recognize the need for forecasts. In Greek mythology, oracles were consulted prior to virtually all major decisions. Many people were dismayed to learn that the Reagans consulted an astrologer.

But most people are not reluctant to take a glance at their horoscopes in the daily newspaper, and thousands, perhaps millions, of people throughout the world regularly consult with psychics, clairvoyants, tarot readers, crystal ball readers, fortune-tellers, the *I Ching*, or tea leaf readers. *Despite this human need to know the future, the future is only minimally predictable.*

Few individuals have demonstrated an ability to predict the future, regardless of the means they employ—technical or occult. Moreover, *it is questionable whether knowledge of the future would guarantee the ability to act on that knowledge.* Perhaps the most potentially serious difficulty that arises as a result of forecasting is that it leads traders to have expectations.

While all of life is built upon expectations, *there are some instances in which an expectation can lead to an unrealistic attitude.* When a light turns green it is reasonable to expect that the opposing traffic will stop for you. This expectation is valid and normal, given the large number of correct repetitions. It is highly unlikely that a green traffic light will fail you. But a market forecast is not like a green light.

A market forecast is nothing but conjecture—it is merely the interpretive opinion of an analyst, an educated guess, or even a wish. A forecast, whether in stocks, commodities, or the economy, is not like a green light. Here are some of my thoughts regarding the dangers of a forecast:

- *A forecast can lead you to expect a certain trend or price target that may not occur.* This may cause you to ignore signals from your trading system(s).

- *Expecting a given price target may cause you to hold a position beyond its ideal exit time.*

- *Traders who have internalized a market expectation based on a forecast may unconsciously avoid trades that are opposite from the forecast.*

- *Traders who use forecasts often read many of them*—if the forecasts disagree with one another, the end result may be a very confused trader.

- *Although a forecast often has the appearance of being based on serious scientific or technical analysis, very often this is not the case.*

- *A forecast must always be considered in terms of the forecaster.* You must always ask whether the forecaster has a bias or a vested interest. This is often the case.

Markets have no respect for forecasts. Markets will do what they want to do when they want to do it. You are far better off following a trend than you are following a forecast.

Fallen Heroes

Some of the best forecasters in the business have ultimately met their defeat at the hands of their prognostications. As an example, consider the history and fate of Robert Prechter, the Elliott Wave wunderkind. Bob rode high upon a wave of publicity with his stock market forecasts; however, once tied to his prediction of a top in the stock market, he stayed with his forecast until it was totally, evidently, and clearly dead wrong.

But I do not single Bob out here for special treatment. I believe Mr. Prechter to be an outstanding analyst and I have deep respect for his work, theories, and philosophies. During the largest and most sustained bull move in stock market history, many a prognosticator has been humbled by a relentless bull market. We are now at the point where most of us are unwilling to predict what the market will do.

I do not consider my forecasts to be the crux or mainstay of my work. It is very likely that my forecasts are ultimately no better than anyone else's. In my many travels the world over I've received literally hundreds of forecasts from taxi drivers, flight attendants, and hotel concierges. Anyone can forecast. Forecasts are like making love—anyone can do it, but few can do it well.

We all have opinions about what the future holds in store. It's impossible to be human and not have an expectation. *But to the trader, expectations are truly anathema. The disciplined trader must do all he or she can to avoid expectations, because, ultimately, expectations will most often lead to disappointments.* Always remember that the dog wags his tail and not vice versa. We cannot wag the market, it must wag us.

How to Break Destructive Trading Habits

The disciplined trader has a distinct advantage over the impulsive trader because impulses and emotions are the trader's worst enemies since they lead to losses. While we all know the dangers of emotional response in the markets, there is a vast expanse of opportunity for error between the recognition of realities and the implementation of programs to diminish or eliminate the repetition of errors.

To put it in plain English, it's wonderful to know that traders make errors due to emotional factors, but it's not helpful to have the knowledge unless you know how to use it.

Awareness

The first step in solving any problem is, of course, to recognize that it exists. In some areas of life it's difficult to know that you have a problem. You keep having bad experiences, you fail at tasks, you have poor relationships, but you can't understand what's going on. You know something is wrong, but you cannot seem to focus on it. This reminds me of Mr. Jones in the Bob Dylan song, "Ballad of a Thin Man." At times we are all in Mr. Jones's situation, though we'd like to be clear on such matters at all times. Once recognized, most problems can be solved.

Fortunately, the trading arena offers virtually immediate feedback when something is wrong. You will lose money when things are *not right* and you will make money when things *are right* (although at times you will make mistakes and still make money).

In other words, when you have an objective way of determining whether you are relating well to the markets, you are more likely to make money. This is fortunate because it provides feedback. Mind you, I am not claiming you will always make money if you have discipline. However, I am saying that your odds of success are considerably greater if you are disciplined. Yet the problem remains one of actually implementing a program to change losing behaviors.

You can say all you want about the academic aspect of problem solving, but none of it will mean a thing unless you can put into action viable solutions to make things happen. While you may not agree with some of my suggestions, do not ridicule them until you have tried them. And if you plan on trying them, give them a fair chance. Don't just try them one time and call it quits if they don't show immediate results.

Simple Behaviors First

Let's begin with a simple, common behavioral problem. Consider the difficulty so many traders have in "pulling the trigger." If you go to a psychiatrist with this problem, you'll end up paying a lot of money for a lot of analysis you don't really need or want.

The simple fact of the matter is that traders are afraid to pull the trigger because they're afraid to lose money. In addition, they are often afraid to enter new positions for fear that the decision will be wrong. This is a very common fear among traders and it is not too dissimilar from the kind of fear many people have when it comes to making important decisions about anything in life that could have negative consequences.

Make a Plan

Let's not analyze it too deeply. The fact is that you're not doing what you are supposed to do because you don't want to make a mistake. One way of dealing with the problem is to accept the fact that you can't make decisions and avoid the temptation to remediate this problem from a psychological level.

To solve the problem dynamically (i.e., psychologically) could take many years. But to solve it behaviorally could take only a few minutes. Say you have a problem pulling the trigger. Let someone else do it for you. *Establish a procedure with a friend or a broker who will place the orders for you.* All you have to do is to sit back and provide the input. It's really a very simple procedure.

16

Putting Your Knowledge into Action

Wine maketh merry: but money answereth all things.

ECCLESIASTES 10:19

At the Push of a Button

The following Kodak advertisement slogan (circa 1888) reminds me of the attitude that so many stock day traders have about their trading nowadays. "You press the button and we'll do the rest."

They feel that making money in the stock market today is as easy as the press of a button. We live in an age of "instantism," in which traders have become spoiled by virtually immediate price fills on orders, quick profits, instant feedback, and soaring profits on IPOs. Most traders have never experienced severe price declines, crashes and mini-crashes, and/or a secular (i.e., long-term) bear market in stocks.

Lacking the experience to trade and psychologically cope with such markets and trends, I fear that many traders could get burned if and when a severe market decline begins. The "press the button" attitude that pervades today's markets could very well prove to be the Achilles heel of tomorrow. My advice to you has been, and remains, as follows:

- *Do not allow yourself to become totally dependent upon the use of electronic order entry.* If the system fails and you can't get your order through, you may very well be stuck with a trade that you *cannot* liquidate as it moves severely against you. I may sound like an alarmist, but, believe me, I'm not. I've lived through many different types of markets and I know whereof I speak. When panic reigns supreme, the existing electronic order processing channels may become overloaded and you may have considerable trouble getting orders filled. I urge you to have a backup method of placing orders. The good old-fashioned telephone is a great backup system. Learn how to use it for order placement and make sure you have a voice backup in place for your online order entry.

- *If you're a day trader, be prepared to exit your positions quickly* (more quickly than usual) at the first sign of a panic liquidation. Even though you may be on the right side of the market (i.e., short), your inability to exit a trade due to a backup of the order entry system will make you wrong.

- *Internet quotes:* Many of you now get your live quotes via the Internet. In the event of a massive stock decline, the Internet will likely cease to be a viable source of communications for a few hours or perhaps even longer. Your quotes may be either delayed, inaccurate, or not delivered at all. *Be prepared* by having a quotation service that is fully reliable or a backup, if you don't want the risk of being quoteless in the event of a panic liquidation.

- *Hedge your portfolio of stocks to include stocks that are currently out of favor.* You can buy low-P/E (price-to-earnings ratio) stocks that have good historical stability but which have not been moving with the market trend.

- *Maintain a high cash position so that if and when a severe decline develops you'll have the money to jump into good-quality stocks at low prices.* Unless you have the available cash to take advantage of the declining prices, you won't benefit even if you correctly anticipated a drop in prices.

"Push of a button" trading is a two-sided coin. On the one hand, it makes for great efficiency and reduced costs. On the other hand, I think that technology in order entry has outgrown what the infrastructure can handle. Sooner or later we may find this out in a very painful way, especially if we aren't ready. So what can you do? Be prepared by following my guidelines.

In Conclusion

I hope that this book has helped you learn a variety of stock day-trading techniques that will help you trade profitably. In an effort to give you various tools, I have presented a number of methods that may be used effectively in your quest for profits.

Some readers may feel that I have given you too many choices in this book. Note that I have done so in order to allow for different trader temperaments and tastes. Traders have different needs, different likes and dislikes, different abilities, and different levels of acceptable risk. Only by having a sufficient selection of alternatives will you be able to choose the method or methods that are best for you.

By now you may already have made your choice(s) or, better yet, you may have been inspired to seek a direction of your own, by using a combination of my ideas and yours. If this is the case, then I am pleased inasmuch as most successful day traders eventually develop their own trading approaches, often drawing from those that are available and synthesizing them into a unique approach.

Before you begin to use any of my methods or any of the methods you develop using my suggestions in this book, *test them as thoroughly as you can*. While it is not always possible to know in advance all of the factors and market conditions that will affect a trading system or method, it is indeed possible to subject the method(s) to a test.

The preferred method is to do so by using historical data and one of the available software programs that have been designed for this purpose. Yet even after such testing it is important to observe and to paper-trade the system or method as a final test of its efficacy and applicability. Some trading systems appear reasonable, logical, and easily implemented when viewed hypothetically on historical data, yet when we attempt to apply them we discover pragmatic limitations. This can only be discovered by a test-drive.

I hope your day-trading experience proves to be a profitable one. Although there are many day traders these days, there are relatively few who use a systematic approach or who practice sound principles of risk management. I believe that by using sound risk management rules you will enjoy a clear advantage over the vast majority of day traders. If I can clarify any of the methods or systems discussed herein, send an e-mail to me. I can be reached at jake@2chimps.com or visit my stock trading web site: www.2chimps.com.

Glossary of Day-Trading Terms

AMEX.   American Stock Exchange.

Analyst.   A brokerage employee who utilizes fundamental and technical analysis to forecast a stock's price, company earnings, and so on.

Ask.   The price at which an individual, group, or firm is willing to sell stock.

Auction market.   A physical market, such as the NYSE and the AMEX, where a specialist acts as an auctioneer, coordinating buying and selling to those making bids and offers.

Bargain hunter.   One who waits for a stock's price to drop or go "on sale" before purchasing it.

Bear market.   When the market retreats 20 percent from its previous high.

Bid/offer.   A *bid* is an offer to buy at a given price, whereas an *offer* is an order to sell at a given price. Buyers bid for a given stock, while sellers offer a given stock, just as you see at an auction. The auctioneer stands at the podium, offering merchandise or goods that have been placed up for sale. The buyers make bids to buy these items at a certain price.

   For example, if a stock is at 45 and you want to buy 100 shares at 43, you would place an order to buy 100 shares at 43 (100S @ 43), which would constitute a bid at 43. If you wanted to sell 100 shares at 47, this would be an offer at 47.

Breakout.   When a stock's price moves past a previous support or resistance level.

Broker.   A salesperson who deals in securities or commodities.

Bull market.   A market in which prices are generally increasing.

Buy and hold.   A strategy involving the purchase of stocks for the long term, typically for years at a time.

Correction.   A less than 20 percent pullback in the market from its previous highs.

Covering a short.   When short sellers repurchase stock to replace or *cover* the stock sold short.

Curve fitting.   *Curve fitting* (or *optimizing*) is the act of fitting a trading system to past data. When a trading system developer optimizes a system, he or she does so in order to generate a set of system rules that have performed well on historical data. Although the system appears to have worked well in the past, it is in fact fitted to the data. Hence, the system will frequently not perform well in the future. To a given extent, most system testing involves some degree of optimization or curve fitting.

Day trade.   A *day trade* is a trade that is entered and exited on the same day. It does not mean that the trade will be held overnight, that it will be kept overnight if profitable, that it will always be entered on the opening and exited on the close, or that it will not entail risk.

Day trades are always over by the end of the trading day. By definition, they are no longer day trades if carried through to the next trading session. Day trades may be entered at any time during the day, but they must be closed out by the end of the day.

Day trader.   A trader who day trades is called a *day trader.* A day trader is not an investor because day trades are not investments. A day trade is a speculation and day traders are speculators.

Whether they do so in stocks, options, futures, mutual funds, currencies, or any other vehicle, a day trade is merely a speculative activity designed to capitalize on intraday price swings.

Day trading.   *Day trading* is trading positions that are entered and exited on the same day.

Downtick.   When the sale price is continuing to fall from a previous fall.

Equity.   Stock; ownership of part of a company by holding the stock of that company.

Fundamental analysis.   An analysis process which looks at the fundamentals or basic issues of a company—price-to-earnings (P/E) ratio, future earnings potential, dividends, income, debt management, market share, and a whole host of other aspects.

Fundamental analysis attempts to determine where a share price *should* be, based on the company's current characteristics and future potential.

Fundamentalist.   Someone who looks at a company's fundamentals to determine where the stock price should be.

Gap.   When a stock's opening price is higher than the previous day's high or lower than the previous day's low.

Intermediate-term trading.   An *intermediate-term trade* is one usually held for several months. Many traders, money managers, and investors prefer such trades.

Intermediate-term traders seek to take advantage of larger price swings but do not wish to hold stocks for several years or more. They seek to maximize their capital by holding stocks for larger moves over a period of months, thereby attempting to capitalize on large market swings.

Investing.   A stock market investor can hold positions for several years or even for many decades. What the day trader does is the antithesis of what the investor does, but with one exception. They both try to make money but they approach the task in distinctly different ways and with markedly different methods.

IPO.   An *IPO* is an *initial public offering* of a stock, or the first time that the general public can purchase shares in a company when it becomes publicly traded.

Level I data.   The highest bid and lowest ask price, or what typical investors get when they call their brokers.

Level II data.   The full table of buyers and sellers of a stock, showing who wants to trade, how many shares they are posting to trade, and at what price they want to trade.

Limit order.   The buyer or seller of a stock sets a maximum price at which he or she is willing to buy, or the minimum price at which he is willing to sell.

Liquid.   A stock that is easily tradable.

Long-term trading.   A *long-term trader* may hold positions for several years, rolling contracts forward as they approach expiration. What the day trader does is the complete antithesis of what the long-term trader does.

Market entry.   *Market entry* means simply to establish a new long or short position. There are many different types of orders that may be used for entering and exiting markets.

Market exit.   *Market exit* means to close out an existing long or short position. Again, there are many different types of orders that may be used for entering and exiting markets.

Market maker.   One of the participants in the NASDAQ market who set stock prices by balancing bids and offers.

Market order.   An order to trade stocks at whichever price happens to be prevailing at the time the order is received.

Market timing.   A strategy that attempts to buy stocks at the bottom of a bear market and sell them at the top of a bull market. This strategy assumes that tops and bottoms can be easily picked.

Momentum.   A combination of volume and volatility in a stock that keeps its price continuing in the same direction.

Momentum indicator.   A mathematical method of quantifying momentum.

Moving averages.   *Moving averages* have many and varied applications in stock trading. Basic application involves buying and selling on penetrations of MA applications, described as follows:

   Simple penetration of MA.   This application is the most elementary. When price closes above a given MA, a buy is triggered. When price closes below a given MA, a sell is triggered.

   MA support/rsesistance method.   Two MAs are used, one about three times the length of the other. The longer MA defines trend. The shorter MA is used for buy and sell points. The text describes detailed techniques more fully.

   10/8 MA channel.   Consists of two MAs, one each of the high and low price, respectively. The 10/8 channel can be used as support or resistance. The 10/8 combination can be used to generate buy and sell points.

NASDAQ.   National Association of Securities Dealers Automated Quotation System.

NYSE.   New York Stock Exchange.

Offer.   A price at which someone is willing to buy stock.

Order flow.   The moment-to-moment incoming buy and sell orders received by specialists and market makers.

Optimization.   The procedure one uses to create a trading system based on historical data is called *optimizing* (or *curve fitting*). A system developer optimizes a system in order to generate a set of system rules that have performed well on historical data.

   Although the system appears to have worked well in the past, it is, in fact, fitted to the data. The given system can be optimized several different ways and, depending upon the method used, the results will have varying degrees of success in their ability to be replicated in the future.

Oscillate.   To *oscillate* is to move back and forth between extremes.

OTC.   *Over the counter*—used for NASDAQ stocks.

Overbought.   After a rapid rally of a stock to prices too high to be sustained, the stock is said to be *overbought,* which could mean that a drop could follow.

Oversold.   After a rapid sell-off of a stock to prices too low to be sustained, the stock is said to be *oversold,* which could mean that a rise could follow.

Overtrading.   Trading simply for the sake of trading and thereby trading too often.

Position.   Holding shares in a certain stock.

Position trader.   As soon as a day trader holds a position overnight, he or she becomes a position trader. A position trader holds trades for an extended period ranging from months to years. The position trader can also be called an *investor* in stocks with a shorter-term perspective.

Position trading.   When day trades are held overnight, they become position trades; therefore, when a trader holds his or her trades longer than a day (i.e., usually months to years) it is called *position trading.*

Profit taking.   When a recent run-up in a stock's price brings sellers onto the market to take profits before the stock moves back down.

Quote.   The current price, bid, and offer on a stock.

Rally.   A rapid run-up in a stock's price.

Resistance.   The price level at which a market is expected to halt its upward trend and from which prices are expected to move lower at best or sideways at worst.

Reversal.   When a stock's price reaches a support or resistance level and turns around from there.

Scalping.   Ultra-short-term trading for very small but intraday profits.

SEC.   Securities and Exchange Commission.

Securities.   Stocks or equities.

Sell-off.   A rapid decline in a stock's price.

Short.   To sell borrowed stock that you do not own in the hope of repurchasing it at a lower price and pocketing the difference.

Short squeeze.   When a stock that many investors have shorted goes up instead, causing the short sellers to have to buy to "cover their shorts," often causing the stock to rally further.

Short-term trader.   A *short-term trader* is one who trades for relatively short-term market swings of 2 to 10 days' duration. There is no firm definition of the exact length of time short-term traders hold their positions.

Short-term trading.   *Short-term trading,* as opposed to day trading or position trading, is trading for relatively short-term market swings of 2 to 10 days' duration. Again, there is no firm definition of the exact length of time for short-term trading.

The distinction between short-term trading and position trading is not as precise as is the distinction between day trading and all other types of trading.

Slippage.   The tendency of a market to fall or rise very quickly, picking buy and sell stop orders very quickly. Hence, a $100 deduction for slippage means deducting $100 from every trade in a hypothetical back-test in order to represent more accurately what might have happened. A market which tends to have too much slippage is, therefore, a market in which quick and sudden price moves tend to result in price fills which are unexpectedly or unreasonably far away from your price orders.

SOES.   Small Order Execution System.

Specialist/market maker.   Acts as an auctioneer in a single stock or in several stocks at auction markets such as the NYSE.

Spread.   The difference between the bid and the ask price.

Stochastics.   The *stochastic indicator* (SI) is basically a price-derived oscillator expressed in percentages. SI values approach 0 and 100 as limits. The SI consists of two values, percent K and percent D. The SI period can be adjusted as desired. The shorter the period, the more the SI will fluctuate.

> **Crossing of 75 percent and 25 percent.**   If one or both SI lines have been above 75 percent and one or both cross below 75 percent on a closing basis for the given period, then sells can be considered. If one or both SI lines have been below 25 percent and if one or both cross above 25 percent on a closing basis, then buys can be considered. Note that a more conservative variation of this application would be to require *both* SI lines to cross as opposed to requiring just one line to cross.

> **Divergence with price.**   If price makes a new high for a given time period but SI does not, then a top may be forming. If price makes a new low for a given period of time and SI does not, then a bottom may be forming.

> **SI pop.**   A buy pop is triggered when one or both SI values close at 75 percent or higher for a given period after having been below 75 percent. A buy pop is exited when the SI lines cross again after the buy pop has been triggered.

> A sell pop is triggered when one or both SI values close at 25 percent or lower after having been above 25 percent. The sell pop is exited when the SI lines cross on a closing basis.

Stock split.   When a stock's price reaches a level that appears expensive to the general public, a company often divides the price but increases the number of shares.

Stop order.   A sell order typically placed just below where a stock's current price is, to enable the seller to exit the stock if a price decline begins or above the current price if one is in a short position.

Support.   The price level at which a market is expected to halt its declining trend and from which prices are expected to move higher at best or sideways at worst.

Tape.   The listing for each stock that gives the time, volume, and price for each sale; same as the old *ticker tape.*

Technical analysis.   Utilizes charts and graphs to determine where a particular stock's price is likely to be headed in the future.

Technician.   Person who uses technical analysis to predict stock trends.

Timing indicators or timing signals.   A *timing indicator* is defined as any specific technique, whether fundamental or technical, which objectively indicates market entry, exit, or the underlying condition (i.e., bullish, bearish, neutral) of a given stock or market index. A timing indicator can also be called a *timing signal,* as the terms are used interchangeably.

Trading range.   Used regarding primarily lateral movement in a stock's price, with limited up and down movements.

Trading systems.   A *trading system* is an organized methodology containing specific market entry and exit indicators, as well as an operational set of procedures (called *rules*), including, but not limited to, various risk management methods (follow-up stop-loss procedures), and procedures. A trading system is implemented by following specific timing signals that dictate market entry and exit.

Trading systems must be necessarily rigid in their construction for the purpose of delineating specific procedures which, theoretically, should lead to profitable trading, provided the system is functioning as intended or tested. A trading system must be systematic or it is not a trading system, regardless of what the individual who professes to be trading a "system" may think.

A few traders actually follow trading systems. The vast majority of traders begin with a system but alter it to suit their internal feelings about the markets to the extent that they are not following a system at all, other than, perhaps, in their own minds.

Trading technique.   A *trading technique* is a fairly loose collection of procedures which assists traders in making decisions about market entry or exit.

Frequently, a trading technique consists of one or more timing indicators, combined with general entry and exit rules and/or risk management procedures. A trading technique is, therefore, not a trading system, but rather an approach to trading which is generally objective but not nearly as precise or rigid as is a trading system.

Trendline.   A line drawn across either the price peaks of a stock trend or the price bottoms, to emphasize the overall trend.

Upbid.   When the bid price is higher than the previous bid price.

Uptick.   When the sales price is continuing to rise after a previous rise.

Volatility.   The price range at which variations in a stock's price occur. The larger the range, the higher the volatility.

Index

About the Author

Jake Bernstein is the author of over 35 market books as well as a 30-year veteran of the stock and commodity markets. He has been a guest on numerous television shows including *Wall Street Week,* appears regularly as a market commentator on radio and television, and has written for a number of prominent financial publications. If you have questions about the systems, methods, or indicators presented in *The Compleat Guide to Day Trading Stocks,* please feel free to write Mr. Bernstein at JAKE@2chimps .com.